Aylesbury Vale Yesterdays

Dedicated to
my Buckinghamshire
Forefathers.

Front endpaper:
THE VALE OF AYLESBURY
from above Aston Clinton
G. C. & M. Farnell

A map of BUCKINGHAMSHIRE, North West from London
Humbly inscribed to his Grace ye Duke of Marlborough
Lord Lieut.t of the County.
According to Act of Parliam.t G Bickham.
1754

Aylesbury Vale Yesterdays

HAYWARD PARROTT

THE
KYLIN · PRESS

Kylin Press Limited,
46 High Street,
WADDESDON,
Buckinghamshire,
HP18 0JA.

First published 1981

Designed by Geoff Apps, Aylesbury
ISBN 0 907128 01 7
Set in AM Bembo
Printed and produced by
Hazell Watson & Viney Limited,
Aylesbury.

CONTENTS

FOREWORD

By Lieutenant Colonel V. H. Band M.C. (Retd.)
Chairman, Aylesbury Vale District Council

THE VALE of Aylesbury is undoubtedly one of the most beautiful areas in England. Those of us who are fortunate enough to live here appreciate the beauty but tend to take its history for granted. This book opens a window onto the past history of the Vale. It is appropriate that it should be written by Mr. Hayward Parrott as the families from which he is descended, the Parrotts and the Haywards, have lived here for many generations and have contributed much to the life of the community during those years.

The book gives intimate details of the life of the people who inhabited the towns and countryside over the centuries. Among the fascinating things are references to all the trades and crafts which used to abound in the area. Many of these trades and practically all the crafts have disappeared from the scene. Mr. Parrott has the gift of bringing the past to life in a most interesting and enlightened way. I am certain that anyone reading this informative narrative will want to visit all the places mentioned. We are also reminded of the part played in history by the Vale and its inhabitants. It makes us realise that the history of the Vale is also to be found in the monuments and records of our Churches.

We are indebted to Mr. Parrott for revealing to us the many events that have shaped life in the Vale of Aylesbury.

PREFACE

I HAVE OFTEN thought that it would be a good idea if someone were prepared to publish, in book form, my articles on mid-Buckinghamshire local history, old houses and the ways of people who lived in them, which have appeared over the years, mostly in county monthlies. This would make them available generally, especially to younger readers at school and college, perhaps kindling a lasting interest and appreciation of the good things from the county's past, how they have evolved and the need to preserve and build on them for the benefit of future generations.

In gathering the substance for my articles, by no means do I claim to be an historian. My interest lies more in the nineteenth and twentieth centuries, to which one can relate through one's forebears – their daily lives, how they earned their living, their home lives and pleasures. I have not spent long hours on original research, most of my material having been drawn from written sources such as early Bucks newspapers, books by local historians, old photographs and personal memories imparted to me by letter or conversation by old Buckinghamshire residents.

It will be noticed that Aylesbury itself is mentioned only incidentally in the text. This is because already in production is a companion volume entitled *'Aylesbury Town Yesterdays'*.

Hayward Parrott

ACKNOWLEDGEMENTS

THE KYLIN PRESS has been established to capture significant events which might otherwise be lost, and to encourage little-known writers who have an important contribution to make.

This certainly applies to Hayward Parrott who, despite a lifetime of research and writing on past local matters, is still not widely known. It has been an honour to work with him.

Over the years he has written extensively in the county magazines, in particular 'Bucks & Berks Countryside'; the author and I would like to thank Mr E. V. Scott, the Editor, for agreeing to these articles being published.

Extensive use has been made of engravings and photographs from Mr Parrott's personal collection. However, others have helped illustrate this book, among them Sister Sale MBE and Mr John Millburn; our thanks to them and the County Reference Library who freely made prints available from 'The Bucks Collection' for reproduction.

Dr & Mrs G. C. Farnell have made an invaluable contribution with some of their own superb photographs, taking a number especially for this book, as well as providing enhanced bromides of old prints.

Our thanks also to Lieutenant Colonel Band for his Foreword and support, and to the many other people who have helped, in any way, to enable 'Aylesbury Vale Yesterdays' to be published.

The Kylin Press
August, 1981

Illustration credits indicate from which collection they come.

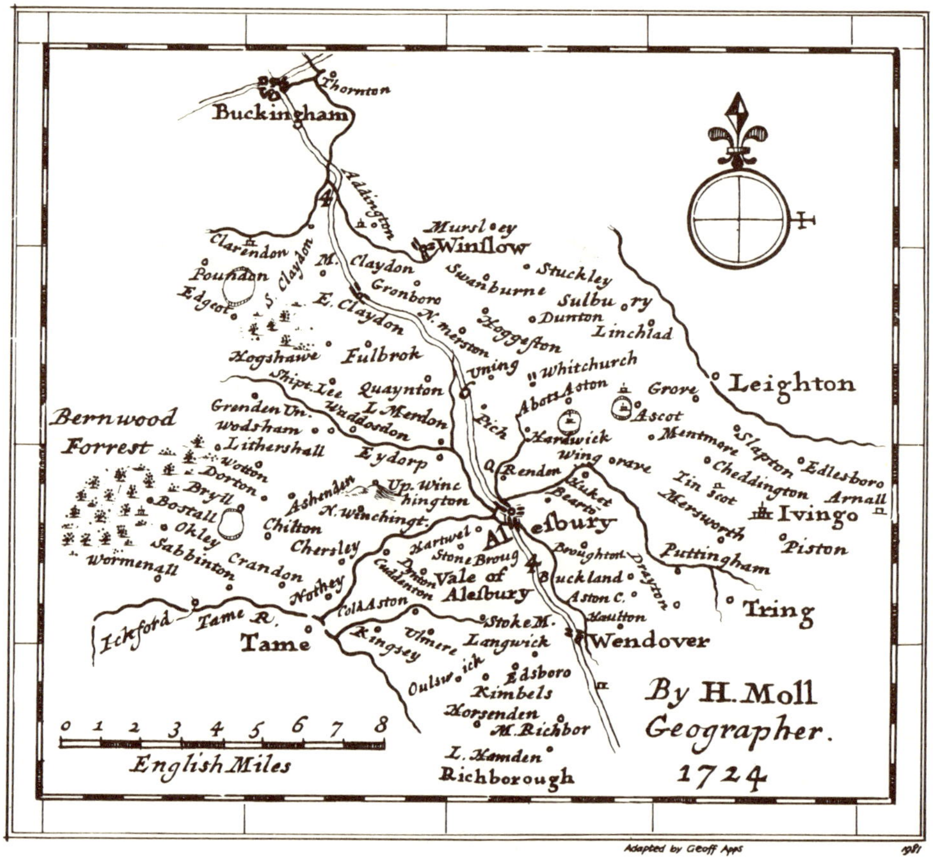

THE VALE OF AYLESBURY
Adapted from a map of Buckinghamshire by H. Moll, 1724

THE VALE OF AYLESBURY

THE AREA of the Vale of Aylesbury has never been clearly defined. John Leland the 16th century antiquary, in his *'Itinerary'* described it as *'going one waye to the forest* (bernwood) *beyond Tame markett; it goeth otherwayes to Buckingham, to Stonye Stratford, to Newport Painell, and along from Aylesbury by the rootes of the Chilterne Hilles, almost to Dunstable.'* On the other hand a Mr. Clare Read writing in 1856, considered the Vale included only Aylesbury, Hartwell, Stone, Winchendon, Waddesdon, Pitchcott, Dunton, Wing, Aston Abbots, Bierton and Broughton, so excluding anywhere south of Aylesbury.

It seems that a generally accepted idea of the extent of the Vale, is to take the Chiltern Hills as the southern boundary, and proceed in a northerly direction to the hilly regions of Brill, Ashendon, Upper Winchendon, Waddesdon, Pitchcott, Oving and Whitchurch. The western edge of the area in between would reach nearly to the Oxfordshire border, and the eastern fringe would be not far from the Bedfordshire border.

Geologically the main portion of the subsoil of the Vale is clay, but the frequent presence of hills of sandy and limestone strata, from which rain washes down material to lighten the clay soil below has been thought to be one of the causes of the great fertility of the Vale, which is well watered by numerous brooks fed by even more rivulets arising from all corners, most of which after following devious courses, pass near Aylesbury and eventually meet and become the River Thame, a tributary of the Thames.

So from time back the area has been known for its agriculture, notably for its preponderence of grazing pastures of which mention of the famous pasture land at Creslow will suffice. On such pastures prize cattle, sheep and pigs have long been bred. Milk production and its products have always been a large part of the farming scene, as also in years past were Aylesbury ducks.

Since the Second World War some of the small towns and villages of the Vale have had new housing estates built on their fringes, some of which are quite large with shopping centres, as at Haddenham. They have changed somewhat from the purely rustic scene of the past. The old communities were close-knit, each having its stone church near the middle, surrounded by stone-built cottages, often thatched and studded with oak beams, the spaces between the timbers being whitewashed.

Beyond lay meadows with buttercups in summer, on which cattle grazed and ambled down to the muddy beaches of the ponds and streams for a drink. Low hills broke the distant view. A church tower or an old Manor House could be glimpsed here and there and roomy farmhouses were scattered almost at random across the Vale.

Over this land long since, huntsmen followed their packs of staghounds, foxhounds and harriers, as well as the beagles, and so they do to-day. Not forgetting the steeplechasers of yore.

The British Museum had rhymes, printed in 1642, in which the stimulating effect of ale from the Vale was held out as *'affecting the parson, the poet, the woer, the widow, the soldier, the sailor, the lawyer, the ploughman, the carter, the reaper, the mower, the thrasher and the sower,'* who all at that time glorified English ale. The following extract gives an idea of the former renown of the potency of the local brew.

Not drunk nor yet sober, but both to a neighbour,
I met with a friend in Aylesbury's Vale;
He saw by my face that I was in the case
To speak no great harm of a pot of good ale.

And as we did meet, and friendly did greet,
He put me in mind of the name of the Dale,
That for Alesbury's sake, some pains I would take
And not burie the praise of a pot of good ale.

Michael Drayton the Warwickshire poet versifies in "Polyolbion" a topographical description of England, published about 1613, concerning the Vale.

For Alesbury's vale that walloweth in her wealth,
And (by her wholesome air continually in health)
Is lusty, firm and fat, and holds her youthful strength.

NO-ONE IS more closely associated with Buckinghamshire and the Vale of Aylesbury than John Hampden (1594–1643). Coming from a line of local squires, he was brought up at the family seat, Hampden House, among the Chiltern beech woods. As a boy, he crossed the Vale on his way to Thame Grammar School and later to Magdalen College, Oxford.

JOHN HAMDEN.

After his marriage in 1619, he settled down at Great Hampden and represented Wendover in the first three parliaments of Charles I. In the Short Parliament (April 1640) and the Long Parliament, he was one of the members for Bucks. At Great Kimble in 1636, he became a national figure by his refusal to pay Ship Money levied on his land in an outlying part of Stoke Mandeville parish. Bucks had been assessed to supply a warship of 450 tons and 160 men, or £4,500 in lieu. Then ensued litigation questioning the legality of Ship Money.

Charles's attempt to arrest Hampden and four other members led to the outbreak of Civil War. Hampden raised his own foot regiment of Bucks men, the *'Greencoats'*, whose motto was *'There is no turning back'*. He took part in the battles with Charles's troops under Prince Rupert's command, which were waged across the Vale, including the Battle of Aylesbury on the 1st November, 1642, and in adjacent counties. Hampden was mortally wounded at the Battle of Chalgrove Field on the 18th June 1643 and died in Thame.

He was buried in Great Hampden Church where there is a monument to his memory. Lord Nugent of *'The Lilies'*, Weedon, near Aylesbury, who had the bones of the soldiers who fell in the Battle of Aylesbury, which were discovered in 1818, removed to Hardwick churchyard and a tomb chest erected, sponsored in 1843 the placing of a momument to John Hampden at Chalgrove Field. In 1863, a Cornish Cross was built on the land near Prestwood on which John Hampden had refused to pay Ship Money. In 1912, a statue of the patriot was unveiled in Aylesbury Market Square.

ANCIENT STONES AT HADDENHAM

GOING THROUGH Fort End, Haddenham, Buckinghamshire, one notices a large unhewn stone in the centre of the open space. A passer-by thought that it had *'something to do with the Romans'* and he was probably correct.

Further inquiry led to Miss Rose, of Grenville Mead, Haddenham, to whom the author is indebted for the following notes concerning this stone and others in Haddenham. Miss Rose kindly produced records collected by her father, the late Mr. Walter Rose, whose books about rural life in Buckinghamshire, and Haddenham in particular, are well-known. Apart from the information which Miss Rose supplied, there appear to be no records concerning these stones.

G. C. & M. Farnell

HADDENHAM
Ancient stone at Fort End

On a map dated 1832 the Fort End stone is marked at the corner of Peakes Lane. Nearby Banks Road takes its name from old earthworks in the vicinity. The stone used to stand opposite the cottage formerly known as the pay-house, where the poor drew parish dole.

The road on which it stood probably formed part of a trackway from the Chilterns, near Chinnor, to Chearsley. This track and others in the area almost certainly existed at the time of the Roman occupation and may well have been in use in even earlier times. Situated near Fort End, it may even have been the council stone marking the spot where the heads of an ancient community were accustomed to hold meetings. In this connection the burial place, or barrow, at Round Hill, near Kings Crossroads, may be significant.

A small upright stone can be seen on the grass verge near to No. 9 Townside, and at least one other lies near the junction of Dollicott and Windmill Road. It seems likely that all these stones, and others since lost sight of, stood in an upright position on their original sites.

Whatever the long story of these ancient stones, it is remarkable that these specimens have survived to this day and not been broken down for road mending or other purposes. Perhaps the largest of the stones, the one at Fort End, might now be enclosed within a railing and a metal plaque attached telling its history.

BOLEBEC CASTLE

FEW WHO drive through Whitchurch, Bucks, know that the earthworks of the ancient castle of Bolebec lie just to the west of the main road. The county seems to have been poorly equipped with fortified castles and of those that existed, mostly in north Bucks, little but their sites remain.

In medieval times Whitchurch must have felt a certain distinction, sheltered as it was by the grey stone walls of the castle and enlivened by the passage of important persons, guests of the Lord of the manor. The castle in their midst provided work and a livelihood for the villagers both within the castle walls and on the manorial estate. As if in recognition of its status, Whitchurch was granted a Monday market in the year 1245 and a fair on the festival of St. John the Evangelist, the patron saint of the 13th century parish church.

To reach the setting of Bolebec Castle, turn off the main road at Market Hill and fork left by Castle Lane which cuts through the centre of the site. The extensive fortifications occupy a commanding position on the hillside with distant views across the Vale of Aylesbury. Half of the castle's bounds now lie within the grounds of Bolebec Placc. The earthworks to the south of Castle Lane can be viewed for public footpaths traverse the site.

On the east side of the castle mound in the field called Lord's Garden is a spring known as *Fair Alice*, named after Alice de Bolebec who reputedly found the waters beneficial. This spring probably joined a part of the moat on the west side known as Weir Pond.

Locally there was said to have been an underground passage running from the castle to the cellars of one of the old houses in the village.

Bolebec Castle may have been erected by a de Bolebec towards the end of the 10th or early in the 11th century in Norman style. But it has also been suggested that it was built during the reign of King Stephen, who encouraged the barons to fortify their estates. He reigned from 1135 to 1154, so the date of erection would have been the first half of the 12th century, in which event the

G. C. & M. Farnell

WHITCHURCH
Bolebec Castle mound is to be seen on the right with ramparts in the mid-ground. Fair Alice rises at a point below the view across the Vale, between the trees

second Hugh de Bolebec, of Norman descent and baron and lord of the manor of Whitchurch, was most probably the builder.

Ample material lay at hand in the local Purbeck limestone. The building consisted of a high outer wall with turrets forming a parapet and outer bailey, the whole being surrounded by a moat crossed only at the tower or motte by a drawbridge. The tower on its mound would provide accommodation for the baron and his family upstairs while the lower floors would be used by servants, and no doubt included a dungeon.

During the Civil War the castle, already in a ruinous state, stood for the Royalist cause and is reputed to have been laid waste by the Roundheads. The castle ruins were regarded by local builders as a fruitful source of ready-hewn stones. They carted them away and incorporated their spoils in the walls of nearby houses and barns. The stone was particularly ideal for the repair of local churches, including that at Wing.

The earthworks have been excavated but little has been found apart from a large stone fireplace complete with embers, a stone conduit which evacuated water from the moat, and human skeletons. Cannon balls have been dug up in the vicinity.

From the Bolebec line the Manor of Whitchurch passed into the hands of the de Vere family by marriage with a Bolebec heiress. Aubrey de Vere was High Sheriff of Bucks in 1129, being killed in a riot in London in 1141. His son was created Earl of Oxford and succeeding Earls of Oxford held the manor until 1548.

Time has largely drawn a veil over the story of Bolebec Castle. There is no record of Royal visits, secret conclaves or conspirators starving in the dungeon. Perhaps in its time Bolebec went on its way without great ado, as Whitchurch does today, while the waters of *Fair Alice's* spring still gush from the earthworks cool to the hand.

IN 1776 *'some villains broke into Quarrendon Church and robbed it of the Communion Plate and linen, viz. a silver cup and cover: upon the cup was engraved "Quarendon" with a Latin inscription which is forgot; they also took a napkin and one breadth of a new surplice which it is supposed was torn off to wrap up the other part of their spoil'.*

Some decades later the beautiful little church dedicated to St. Peter, at Quarrendon just north of Aylesbury, was falling into decay; the process being speeded by marauders looking for stone and pilferers for pieces of monuments which they could turn into ornaments. The chapel was mentioned in a document dated 1266 and was for long an appendage of Bierton church. It was restored by Sir Henry Lee who also founded an adjacent 'hospital'.

Sister Sale MBE

S.E.VIEW of QUARENDON CHAPEL,
Buckinghamſhire.

The manorial lands of Quarrendon being sparsely inhabited, the church depended largely on the nearby mansion, the residence of Sir Henry Lee, champion to Queen Elizabeth. Here the Society of Knights Tilters assembled in arms each November and held a tourney. On Sir Henry's resignation from office the Queen paid him a royal visit. She was regaled with '*gorgeous entertainment*' and a masque was performed for her. The mansion was pulled down early in the 18th century.

Interior VIEW of QUARENDON CHAPEL, Bucks.
looking East.

Sir Henry Lee was born in 1531 and had been a page to Henry VIII. He was a Privy Councillor and was knighted in 1553, becoming a Knight of the Garter in 1597. He was lord of the manor of Fleet Marston and Quarrendon, and twice represented Buckinghamshire in Parliament. He founded Aylesbury Grammar School about 1598 with an endowment of £8 a year.

In 1817 Dr. Lipscomb, the county historian, reported the dilapidated state of the church and mutilation of the monuments. The place was strewn with fragments of statues, cornices and marbles. In the chancel were remains of a magnificent altar tomb on which was the recumbent effigy of a Knight of the Garter, in alabaster, with an inscription to Sir Henry who died in 1611 *'after having served five succeeding princes with a body bent to earth and a mind erected to heaven'*.

The Mirror, a contemporary periodical, described the monument as *'supported with surcoats and helmets, and adorned with banners, battle-axes and javelins. On it is a figure of the Knight in Complete armour with a surcoat, collar and George of the Order of the Garter; his head reposing on a helmet adorned with a plume of feathers'*. Black marble tablets bore lengthy inscriptions in Latin and old English.

There was also the fine tomb of Sir Anthony Lee and his wife Margaret, parents of Sir Henry. Offers to remove the surviving monuments to *'The Lilies'* at Weedon or the chapel at Hartwell were frustrated.

For a time there was another tomb to Anne Vavasour, one of the Queen's maids of honour, with whom when about sixty Sir Henry Lee fell in love with and took to live with him. Her tomb bore this inscription:

Under this stone entombed lies a fair and worthy Dame,
Daughter to Henry Vavasour, Anne Vavasour her name.
She living with Sir Henry Lee for love long time did dwell,
Death could not part them, but here they rest within one cell.

Within a year or two of Sir Henry Lee's death, Anne Vavasour's tomb had been *'erased and pulled down'*, as a mark of displeasure, with or without ecclesiastical authority.

Sir Henry Lee's legal wife was buried at Aylesbury, her tomb in the parish church being well-known.

The question of preserving the chapel ruins was raised by the Archaeological Society in 1856.

Warning notices had been posted to deter further desecration; arms and legs of monuments had been used for propping up pigsties. Soon the south porch was levelled and much of the south wall of the nave had fallen. The east wall had been excavated. The chancel arch had been picked away leaving the wall above unsupported. It was feared that if nothing was done little would be left to save.

A piece of stone from the ruins of the old church has been built into the wall of the modern district church of St. Peter on the nearby Quarrendon estate in Aylesbury, thus preserving a link with the ancient church at Quarrendon.

G. C. & M. Farnell

QUARRENDON

The Chapel as it appeared in the early part of this century

ICKFORD CHURCH AND BRIDGE

ICKFORD LIES among the low meadows on the Buckinghamshire side of the River Thame where it forms a natural boundary between that county and Oxfordshire. The village church should be visited not only by the antiquarian but also by the admirer of good modern stained glass, the wood carver and the man who understands the mysteries of wheels and pulleys. For good measure look back and see who has occupied the Rectory in past years. One senses a rectorial tradition that has woven itself around the mainly thirteenth-century church of St. Nicholas.

Hayward Parrott

ICKFORD
The Church

Among many noteworthy features the monument in the chancel to Thomas Tipping, 1595, and Margaret his wife and their nine children, is outstanding. Between the lower columns are two panels each with kneeling figures in low relief of their four sons and five daughters, bearing over their heads the initials of their Christian names: girls *I – F – A – E – M;* boys *B – G – B – W.* Above these there is the inscription plate with a large strapwork

G. C. & M. Farnell

surround; quaint figures with Red Indian head-dresses climb about the strapwork; according to Dr. Nikolaus Pevsner's *'Buckinghamshire'* these are a tradition of Flemish ornamental prints. Over all is the family shield with arms.

Also to be seen are the fourteenth-century saddle-back roof, a series of Elizabethan benches almost in their original state and a Jacobean pulpit with original centre post and a tester. The west singers' gallery has Caroline panelling on the front and is supported by two columns. The small Early English lancet window in the north aisle contains all that is left of the ancient silvered quarries which were re-leaded and placed there in 1907.

Turning to the modern stained glass, the following windows bear Sir John Ninian Comper's motif, the strawberry leaf and fruit:

- Late Norman window in the north aisle with portrait of Sir Thomas More, Chancellor of England and martyr, dedicated in praise and thanksgiving for deliverance from the perils of war, 1939–1945.
- Fourteenth-century window in north aisle with three cinque-foiled lights under a square head. Each light contains a figure, the centre one being that of the Virgin and Child; over each figure is a medallion. This glass was inserted in memory of Edward Vernon Staley, 2nd Lieut. R.F.A., who fell in the battle of Epēhy, France, on September 18, 1918, aged 19 years.
- East window in north aisle, a paired lancet depicting figures of the Venerable Bede and St. Dunstan, Archbishop of Canterbury. This was placed in memory of Vernon Staley, Rector 1911–1933, Honorary Canon and sometime Provost of Inverness Cathedral, writer and craftsman.

It was Canon Staley who carved most of the modern church furniture. The remarkable *'steeple'* font cover of open trellis work, in oak, and seven feet high, dates from about 1916. This is raised by means of a pulley. (The font cover at nearby Brill is also Canon Staley's work.)

Other work by Canon Staley is the small lectern under the west gallery, and one feels that the wooden candlesticks by the 1914–1918 war memorial tablet must be his work as well as the high altar candlesticks which are dedicated to his son. There is also much restoration at his hands to the older furniture of the church.

Canon Vernon Staley (1852–1933) was by all accounts loved by all with whom he came in contact, humble in his way of life in the best Christian tradition but a man of learning who wrote numerous religious books, among which *'The Catholic Religion'*, a manual of instruction for Anglicans, was long regarded as a standard work. Canon Staley's remains lie with those of his wife at the south-east corner of the churchyard near the Calvary mounted on a tall slim column of wood, carved by him, erected in 1915.

Vernon Staley's important work *'The Life and Times of Gilbert Sheldon'* appeared in 1913. Gilbert Sheldon (1568–1677) became rector of Ickford in 1636, having been elected Warden of All Souls', Oxford, the previous year when he was already Chaplain-in-Ordinary to King Charles I. Sheldon continued to occupy the rectory until his preferment to the See of London in 1660. He was made Archbishop of Canterbury three years later. It was, of course, Sheldon who spent £25,000 on building the Sheldonian Theatre in Oxford. During the plague of 1665 as Bishop of London he remained faithfully at his palace at Lambeth, when all who could do so had fled from London. When victims of the plague were dying all round the palace he ministered to their needs from his own pocket. In 1661 Sheldon presented massive Communion plate to his old parish of Ickford. Made of silver, the cup is 9½ inches high and has a diameter of 5½ inches at the lip. The paten, which can also be used as a cover to the cup, rests on a shallow circular foot. The weight of the vessels is recorded in the Ickford register for 1730:

'Cup, 23 oz. 10 dwt. 12 grs. Cover, 9 oz. 3 grs.'

A quarter of a century after Sheldon left Ickford, the bridge across the River Thame on the Tiddington road was re-built. It consists of three tri-centred arches on heavy stone piers. On each side of the bridge, facing up and down stream between the two northern arches, is a cutwater. The cutwaters are carried up to the coping and form a V-shaped niche on each side. In the eastern niche on the south side is a stone inscribed: *'1685, Here ends the County of Oxon;'* and on the north side a stone inscribed: *'Here beginneth the County of Bucks, 1685.'*

According to old records, a bridge existed here as early as 1237, in which year Walter de Burgh was ordered to provide the keeper of Ickford Bridge with an oak from Brill Wood for repairs.

WILD BOARS roamed the forests of Britain thousands of years before the Middle Ages. Strong muscular animals, fast and savage when cornered, they were obvious prey for the hunter in search of sport and meat for his board. In Britain they died out in the 16th century but are still found in marshy wooded areas of central Europe and elsewhere.

Centuries ago, large parts of Buckinghamshire which are now cultivated were forest tracts made up of woodland, thicket and waste, the natural home of wild beasts. Gradual reclamation of the forests for agriculture deprived the wild pigs of shelter and protection and cut down their sources of food: beech mast, acorns, crab apple, wild plums and bracken roots. These forces coupled with the toll of the hunters eventually overwhelmed the wild species in Britain.

The European wild boar has a thick undercoat of soft curly hair with long bristles thrusting through to form an outer covering, and powerful tusks. It is dark brown or grey-black and the sow farrows four to six young which are brown with white spots and stripes. The adult is generally bigger than the usual domesticated hog, its legs much longer and more muscular and its back higher, having no superfluous fat or flesh. Their strong jaws and tusks could maim their enemies, while powerful forequarters made them formidable in battle.

Men usually hunted on horseback armed with long-handled spears; but at times they hunted on foot, aided by hounds which goaded the boars as they broke from cover and often lost their lives after being savaged by a boar's tusk. In Europe, the boar is still hunted with dogs but the spear except in case of emergency and for the final thrust, has been superseded by the gun.

In the Middle Ages, the Forest of Bernwood covered a large part of north west Buckinghamshire. Here Nigel, a famous forester, is said to have slain a huge wild boar, the terror of the countryside, which had disrupted hunting parties arranged by King Edward the Confessor while at the Royal Palace at

The Plan of BORSTAL.

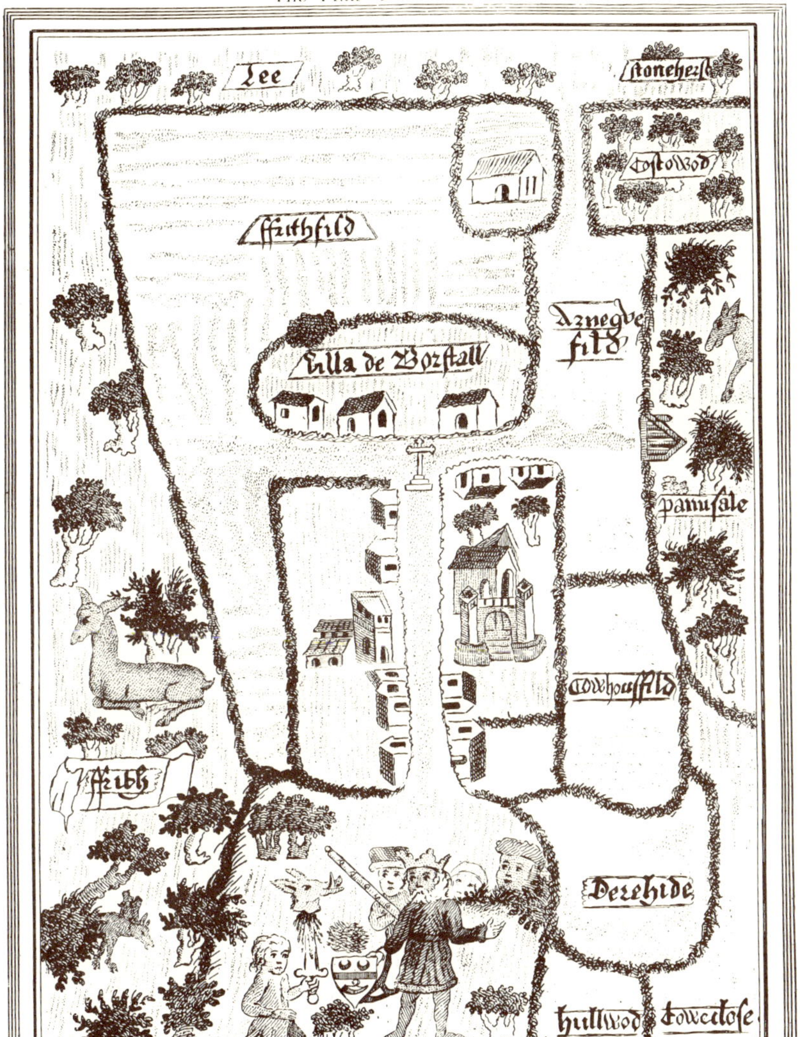

The Bucks Collection

nearby Brill.

In recognition of deliverance from this fearsome beast, the King granted to Nigel and his heirs a part of the forest woodland at Boarstall, near Brill, the name has no connection with a boar; and appointed him custodian of the Forest of Bernwood while keeping for himself rights of vert (cover for deer) and venison.

The Monarch also presented Nigel with a great horn having a leather thong to hang round the neck. What is thought to be the original horn still exists. It is highly polished and dark brown in colour and is 2 ft. 4 in. long, the larger end being 3¾ in. across. It is embellished at the ends and round the centre with bands of silver gilt. An old brass ring bearing a crude imprint of a horn and a brass plaque similarly engraved and four small medallions accompany the horn.

By a Chartulary of King Henry the VIth dated 1440, a Shield of Arms was granted to the hunter's family and their descendants, showing the King presenting Nigel with a shield while the hunter bears the boar's head impaled on a sword. The boar is one of the four Heraldic beasts of the chase.

Nothing remains of the 14th century mansion at Boarstall except the embattled gate-house tower approached across the old moat. Now National Trust property, it is not open to view. Boarstall played a prominent part when Sir William Campion, the Royalist, was besieged therein by Sir Thomas Fairfax, Commander in Chief of the Parliamentary army during the Civil War.

Today the scattered village is a haven of peace. The Wild boar has lost the battle for existence. The sound of cannon balls is heard no more at Boarstall Tower.

THE BOARSTALL HORN

DODDERSHALL

DODDERSHALL WAS originally one of three old manors in the parish of Quainton, Buckinghamshire. It is thought that there was a house on the site at least 1,000 years ago, and in medieval times it is said to have belonged to a family which gave it its name; early records referring to Dodder's Hall.

In 1503 it passed by purchase to Thomas Pigott of Whaddon, Bucks, serjeant at law, and continued in that line of the family until 1735 when the estate descended to a Shropshire branch. The house has remained in the same family since the days of Serjeant Pigott.

Doddershall is even now rather tucked away (up to 100 years ago there were no roads there) and harbours a hint of secrecy. It is not a great county mansion, but is full of character, with much historical and architectural interest. Moreover, it has been a family home down the centuries.

The building stands on three sides of a quadrangle, of which the oldest side is thought to date from the time of Richard II. Two crude sculptured figures in medallions on the chimney stack are thought to represent the king and his queen, Anne of Bohemia. The Pigott family crest of three pickets is also represented – it is a pun on the name.

Drinking water was drawn from a spring in the cellar of the south west wing, which was built towards the close of the 17th century. Prior to that the well stood in the open, yielding a constant supply of good water. The celebrated politician John Wilkes, of Aylesbury, presented a bell for the roof. Part of the ancient moat remains on two sides.

It is related that Serjeant Thomas Pigott's widow put in hand alterations to the house which involved her in a legal action concerning the timbers she had used. It was contended that they should have been put at the disposal of the naval ship builders. However, she was able to prove that she had acquired them in good faith as free wood. The timbers were used in the Stone Hall.

Doddershall has its share of trap doors, secret passages and hidden rooms. Old spits and wooden hooks for hanging hams, hang from the old kitchen ceiling. Apart from an ancient oven there is an old elm side-table, a salt cupboard and a small cupboard for spices.

The staircase banister rails are traditionally thought to have been the communion rails from the long vanished Hogshaw church near Quainton. They are supported by strong twisted balusters, while the panelling in the Chapel Room was made from the old doors to the former box pews in Quainton church.

Perhaps the most picturesque of the former holders of Doddershall was Christobella Pigott, widow of John Pigott, who died in 1751. She took as her third husband the sixth Viscount Saye and Sele, who died in 1781. Lady Saye and Sele held the estate until her death in 1789 at an extremely advanced age.

The Bucks Collection

DODDERSHALL

The Bucks Collection

DODDERSHALL

Attributed to her is the remark that she contrived to secure a good partner by an annual present of a side of venison to a gentleman who danced remarkably well; but that she began to think he seemed to like younger ladies better and believed she must increase her bribe to a whole buck, that she might *'not lose so agreeable a partner'*. She said that she had chosen *'her first husband for love, her second for riches, and her third for honours'* and that she *'had now some thought of beginning again in the same order'*.

It was Christobella, Viscountess Saye and Sele, who in her will dated 1787, left money to found a charity. By a court order in 1850 schools were established in Grendon and Quainton and annual apprenticeships were set up for boys from these villages, with the charitable funds.

BROUGHTON MANOR FARM

BROUGHTON MANOR farmhouse has ancient origins, for it is recorded that the manor of Broughton, which is in the parish of Bierton, near Aylesbury, and once formed part of the propery of the dissolved Missenden Abbey, was granted by Henry VIII in 1540 to Sir John Baldwin. Sir John, who was favoured by the king, sometimes lived at Aylesbury, benefiting the town by building causeways and improving nearby roads.

In the same year it is stated that the king also transferred the manor, most probably this referred to another parcel of the manor estate, to Michael Dormer, a forebear of Baron Dormer of Wing. In 1672 the manor, then called Broughton Abbots, was conveyed by Edward Backwell of London and others to Henry Johnson of Blackwall, Middlesex, and in 1801 the estate was sold by Sir John Pakington to the Marquis of Buckingham.

In 1832 the manor of Broughton Abbots, comprising a large farmhouse and outbuildings plus 141 acres of pasture land together with other land in Broughton as well as Broughton water mill and the miller's house, was vested in the trustees of Aylesbury Grammar School.

This investment had been made possible by the legacy of £5,000 received under the will of Henry Phillips who died in 1714, for the enlargement of and provision for the Free School in Aylesbury, the money to be invested in land and the income arising from it to be applied to the education of poor boys of Aylesbury and Walton.

The old farmhouse shows signs of its ancient origins and is situated behind the adjacent Broughton Mill. It used to have a moat often filled with water, crossed by a bridge which has since been removed. At one time an old projecting porch survived. Foundations of a building were found in a field nearby which were thought to have been the site of the original Broughton chapel.

During most of the last century and well into this, Broughton Manor was farmed by three generations of the Roads family. An 1854 directory lists Mr.

Hayward Parrott

BROUGHTON
The Manor Farm and moat

Thomas Roads as being there then and his grandson, Mr. T. J. Roads, was there until fairly recent times.

An unusual and interesting feature of Broughton Manor Farm was the late eighteenth or early nineteenth century horse-driven wooden churn. The main gear wheel, from which hung an iron fork which fitted the horse's saddle, was in an upper room. The horse walked round beneath the wheel, turning it as he went.

The wheel engaged with a smaller wheel in the room below, which turned a shaft with a larger crown-wheel on to which was geared a pinion linked to the axle which turned the churn. In 1848 there were two such churns which were used twice weekly, producing forty-six pounds of butter.

The Bucks Collection

BROUGHTON
The horse-driven churn, in its original setting

BROUGHTON
The horse-driven churn, seen at the Science Museum, Kensington

The dairy was part of the farmhouse and was accessible from the churnhouse. In Mr. T. J. Roads' time there were twenty-two leads for setting the milk and a lead cistern for the cream. At one time he sent sixty dozen pounds of butter by carrier to London weekly. One cowhouse was at the farm and another over a mile distant in a field called *Callage* from which the milk was carried in big wooden buckets on a yoke. Mr. Thomas Norwood of Bierton who worked for Mr. T. J. Roads' grandfather used to get up at 4 am and lived to be over ninety.

Mr. T. J. Roads presented the old wheel and churn to the Science Museum at South Kensington. The building which housed it had to be pulled down to get it out, and the wheel was cut in four pieces and lifted over the moat for its journey to London where it was reassembled.

LADY DODD'S almshouses were built in 1746 on land south of Ellesborough Church, Buckinghamshire. They abut on to an old road leading to Chequers Court, known as the Coach Road.

Dame Isabella Dodd by her will dated 1720 left £2,500 to trustees to be invested in property, the income of which was to be spent in buying a site and erecting an almshouse with convenient apartments for old men and old women, lame or blind or of the poorest inhabitants of Ellesborough, or places adjoining. Provision was made for weekly allowances for the inmates and the supply of fitted gowns every two years.

In 1747 the trustees invested £1,000 in land at the Friarage and Haydon Field in Aylesbury. Further sums were laid out on the purchase of a house and land at Kimblewick and meadows at Tansy Hill, Great Kimble. An inscription on the almshouses records their erection in 1746, the founder being a daughter of Sir Robert Croke of Chequers, one time MP for Wendover, and the widow of Sir Samuel Dodd, Lord Chief Baron of the Exchequer.

The report of the Charity Commissioners dated 1833 stated that the building was divided into four dwelling-rooms, which have four doors, two of which open into a large hall in the centre and two into the back kitchen; to each of these dwelling-rooms there is a wood-room attached; there is also the hall and back kitchen, and a garden containing about a quarter acre, which is divided into allotments.

In the back kitchen there is still an old Board of Rules defining the conduct of the tenants, breach of which could mean loss of allowance or in dire cases, expulsion.

In 1883 inmates received 3*s* 6*d*. a week each, and 2*s* 6*d*. at Christmas; men had a coat and women a gown and petticoat once in two years, at Christmas.

The dwellings were thoroughly restored and modernised about 1955, largely as a result of the successful appeal for funds conducted by the then rector of Ellesborough, the Rev. C. N. White, who personally wrote over 500 letters in copperplate style and sent them all over the world. Each letter took him fifteen minutes to write and he replied personally to everyone who answered with or

G. C. & M. Farrell

ELLESBOROUGH

Lady Dodd's Almshouses are in the foreground with the Church and the Vale of Aylesbury beyond

LADY DODD'S ALMSHOUSES, ELLESBOROUGH

RULE 1. (Marriage entailed expulsion).

RULE 2. That all the men and women shall dispose themselves to do such work as they could do, and not live idle if able and in health, that by some labour they might get something to keep themselves when sick.

RULE 3. That none should lodge with them in their chambers, or lye with them upon any pretence whatsoever, but everyone to help the other by turns when sick or otherwise, being under one roof, as in charity they ought to do, and in case anyone else helps them, they are not to lodge there. But that none of them should lye out of the almshouse nor Wander, nor Beg Alms upon any pretence whatsoever, upon pain of expulsion.

RULE 4. (This governs the payment of weekly allowances after attendance at church service. Absence except for illness entailed forfeiture of half the allowance.)

RULE 5. If anyone Dies before the year expires, their gown to go to the next that comes in.

RULE 6. If anyone of them curse or swear, or scold or make a brawling, or quarrel, for ye first offence shall forfeit half a week's allowance, for the second shall forfeit ye whole week's allowance, to go towards the repairs of the house, and for the third shall be expelled.

RULE 7. If any man or woman sit in an Alehouse for above half an hour or frequent Ginn shops, upon the Oath of one credible witness, shall forfeit one whole week's allowance for the first offence, second expulsion.

RULE 8. They shall forfeit one shilling each time they miss receiving the sacrament when administered in Ellesborough church.

RULE 9. All the inhabitants to eat together in the hall, when well, and each to club or labour to get fuel to burn in the Hall in Common for them all.

RULE 10. The Inhabitants never to be seen without their gown.

ELLESBOROUGH
The Almshouses

without a donation enclosed.

There are four tenants in occupation today. Happily no tenant has been expelled within living memory. The gardens of the almshouses present a vivid show of flowers to the many people who pass by on their way to explore the Chiltern Hills towards Chequers Court.

THE QUAINTON THORN

THE RECTORY garden at Quainton, Buckinghamshire, presented a strange spectacle on Christmas Eve 1753. At midnight crowds from the village and countryside trampled the lawns and flower beds swinging torches and lanterns. They had come to witness the budding of the holy thorn which was said to have grown from a slip of the famous thorn at Glastonbury. The holy thorn was reputed to bud each year on Christmas Eve so as to be in full bloom on Christmas Day.

In 1753 *(new style)* this flowering had a special significance for the inhabitants. In 1752 England adopted the Gregorian reform of the Julian calendar, which was then eleven days out. September 2 was suddenly followed by September 14. No wonder the people cried *'Give us back our eleven days.'* In the rural areas indignation was intense. To the countryman it seemed that Parliament was interfering with the natural order of things. It was robbing the people of eleven days.

At Quainton feeling ran high. The crowd in the rector's garden that Christmas Eve sought proof that Parliament had no power to upset the calendar. Would the holy thorn bud at Christmas Eve (*old style*) or would it agree with the new style calendar? If the rector's bush budded at midnight on December 24 (*new style*), by the laws of man and nature the day after would be the true Christmas Day.

The thorn did not show any sign of budding. This proved beyond doubt that the next day was not the true Christmas Day. People avoided going to church and shunned festivities. To still the clamour Christmas services were held in the country churches on old Christmas Day (*January 5*). Christmas feasts were held in Quainton homes as in their fathers' time. Parliament could do what it liked.

The Glastonbury thorn from which the thorn at Quainton was said to have derived was traditionally linked with Joseph of Arimathaea, who came on a mission to Britain. Arviragus, king of Britain, granted him a piece of land to

The Bucks Collection

QUAINTON
The Old Rectory

build a church. When Joseph came to Weary-all-Hill by Glastonbury he thrust his staff into the ground. The staff was said to have put forth leaves and the next day was in bloom. Henceforth this tree always bloomed on Christmas Eve. Slips thereof planted in other places invariably bloomed on the same day. The blossoms became regarded as infallible remedies for all ills. Their healing virtues became so well known that in the time of Henry VIII Bristol merchants exported them to Europe.

The Glastonbury thorn grew up with twin trunks. In Queen Elizabeth's time a Puritan axed one of the trunks, and the other was destroyed at a later time. Although the tree was supposed to have been dead more than a century, a great crowd arrived to see it bloom on Christmas Eve 1753 (*new style*). As at Quainton, they were disappointed. When old Christmas Eve came round on January 5 it was said to have bloomed as usual. Old Christmas Day must be the true one.

The holy thorn was a fairly common object. Slips of the Glastonbury thorn had been planted in many places. At Dillington, near Ilminster, country folk believed that on Christmas Eve the cattle went down on their knees before the holy thorn. In West Devon and elsewhere it was commonly believed that at midnight on Christmas Eve the oxen in their stalls went down on their knees in an act of devotion to the holy Child and continued to do so after the alteration of the calendar, on the eve of old Christmas Day. This is sometimes seen in old prints of the nativity.

A holy thorn at Woodham Ferrers, Essex, was reported to have burst into leaf before a great crowd on old Christmas Eve towards the end of the nineteenth century and resumed its normal condition within a few hours. This thorn had been imported from Palestine.

The holy thorn in the churchyard of St. John's church, Glastonbury, claimed to be an offspring of the original thorn, began to open on Christmas Eve 1950, leaves, berries, buds and half-opened blossom appearing together on its boughs.

The most likely explanation is that the oriental thorn blooms naturally about Christmas time and in a mild winter asserts its habit in this country. The parishioners of Quainton no longer invade the garden of the old rectory on Christmas Eve be it by old style or new style.

GOOSEBERRIES AND TEETOTALLERS

THE GOOSEBERRY SOCIETY met regularly each season at *'The Bugle Horn'* at Hartwell, Bucks, in the 1840's and 1850's. Here members produced their most weighty fruits, the heaviest gooseberry taking first prize. After the exhibition they all sat down to dinner, presided over by the renowned Dr. Lee of Hartwell House, who brought some friends from London to join the gardeners of Hartwell and Stone, who also received prizes for the best cultivated gardens.

Some members came from Aylesbury, including Mr. J. K. Fowler, famous host of the old White Hart Hotel in the Market Square. Mr. Fowler related that a cottager would bemoan that his *'Gunner'* was *'busted'*. Another was woeful because a *'London'* had rotted.

Size and weight carried the day. Bushes would be planted two or three years before the fruit it gave was fit to be exhibited. Pruning, manuring and thinning out followed until three or four gooseberries only remained. So if anything *'bust'* on the actual day, it spelt disaster after the long preparation that had gone on before.

Each gooseberry was weighed by the judges. Four colours, red, green, yellow and white each received coveted prizes. The premier prize of a copper tea-kettle was awarded to the grower of the heaviest berry in the show. These always exceeded 20 dwt, and once a red London reached 27 dwts.

Dr. Lee took the chair at the dinner. Being teetotal he and some of his friends drank the toasts in water. This drink he praised highly as it came from the spring at Hartwell known as the Egyptian Spring which is protected by a stone covering bearing a carving which is said to mean '*Water is best*'. However, despite Dr. Lee's presence, the main company drank and smoked to their hearts' content.

It was Dr. Lee and his friends who in the 1840's erected the Egyptian style structure at Hartwell spring. The old Turnpike road from Aylesbury to Oxford going through Hartwell passed by the spring. One day over a hundred people going to Aylesbury market were seen to drink at the spring, to the lament of Mr. Joseph Carter at *'The Bugle'*, many of whose customers no longer called in for a beer.

Dr. Lee's edict that water was best, was given expression every summer by a monster gathering of teetotallers in Hartwell Park. About noon the Long Crendon band headed a procession of teetotallers and Rechabites from Aylesbury. At the park, cricket, picnic parties, and *'healthful recreation for all classes'*, including country dances and quadrilles, kiss-in-the-ring and rural sports, went on until dark, interspersed by speeches from the delegates who lodged at Hartwell House which was thrown open by the doctor. An ample table was the rule there although vegetarians and anti-smokers were allowed alcoholic refreshment. Dr. Lee was broadminded evidently regarding others' beliefs.

Mr. Carter at *The Bugle* picked up a deal of trade at festival times. Allied with the 'anti' societies' junketings was the Universal Peace Society's demonstration under its champion Elihu Burritt, an inspired blacksmith, and other noted Americans.

It was said that when Joe Carter called at the mansion with his rent, Dr. Lee enquired after trade at the inn. Carter reported that it was bad owing to his regulars taking to heart the words they had heard at the Temperence Festival. Dr. Lee was so delighted that he refunded the rent as compensation. In fact the licensee always stocked up with his famous home-brewed beer and his nut-brown ale, plus gallons of spirits, for the festival, and sent urgent calls daily to Aylesbury for extra barrels.

So the villagers of Stone and Hartwell could take their pick of these societies in the 1840's and 1850's. Perhaps most of them preferred the Gooseberry Society, membership of which did not entail abstention at the annual dinner at *The Bugle*. What matter then if someone's *'Gunner'* had ***'busted'***.

NOWADAYS ANYONE who asks the way to Halton would be directed to Halton Camp, beneath the Chilterns near Wendover. Such is the fame of the Royal Air Force No. 1 School of Technical Training, that it has taken under its wing the old village from which the camp gets its name.

Placed between two main roads to London, traffic through the village is mostly service vehicles and leisurely drivers on their way to watch the gliders over the airfield. Most village houses carry reminders of the de Rothschild era which began when Baron Lionel de Rothschild bought the manor about 1851.

In 1884, his son Mr. Alfred Charles de Rothschild built nearby Halton House in French chateau style. Mr. de Rothschild exercised benevolent tutelage over his tenants, most of whom worked on the estate or in the mansion. Their village homes were embellished with arms and monograms, and had plaster pictures of the four seasons, woodcutters and rural craftsmen. It is hard to find a house which dates certainly before the de Rothschild era.

Hayward Parrott

HALTON

Looking down towards the old humped back bridge which spanned the Grand Junction Canal (Wendover Arm). Now replaced by a low, sweeping, modern bridge

No doubt arises on this score about the church which was rebuilt in 1813. Inside there is a brass to Henry Bradshawe who died in 1553, a former lord of the manor who became Chief Baron of the Exchequer. He is in robes of office, kneeling at a desk, his wife Joan opposite to him, wears a gown with epaulets and ruffles. Behind them are their children. This, with the Communion Plate, have survived from the earlier building. The churchyard in its peaceful setting is beautifully tended. Many men who have served in the Royal Air Force lie within its boundaries.

At the end of the 18th century the Wendover arm of the old Grand Junction Canal was opened, cutting through the middle of Halton village, under a steep and narrow road bridge. In December 1799 there passed underneath it a prize ox weighing 241 stone, on a two day's voyage by barge to the first Smithfield Fat Stock Show in London. The waterway being no longer used, the bridge, for long a familiar feature, was demolished in 1967. The new bridge does away with the dangerous hump in the road.

Hayward Parrott

HALTON
The Annual Show in full swing

G. C. & M. Farnell

Some way from the village, at the corner of Halton Lane, there stands a house which was rebuilt from two cottages. This used to be *'The Golden Perch'*. The inn was aptly named as it was adjacent to Halton reservoir which was formed by the canal company to control the water level in the canal.

Further west on the road from Aylesbury to Wendover, is the house which for long served as the Rectory. The Rev. C. E. Roberts conducted there for many decades a small 'prep' school. Up to the 1920's the boys clad in Eton suits and top-hats, walked the mile or so, to attend Sunday services at church, where some of them sung in the choir.

The men of Kitchener's army pitched tents below the great beechwoods of Halton during the First World War. The camp was plagued by mud and illness. Later came the Royal Flying Corps, fore-runners of the R.A.F. Tents were replaced by brick barrack blocks. The first entry of Aircraft apprentices arrived in 1922. The R.A.F. took over every corner of the old de Rothschild estate, including its great mansion. Old Halton village, too, came under its protective wings.

DORTON SPA

THE MINERAL springs rising round Brill in north-west Buckinghamshire had long been known. One of these at Dorton achieved passing fame in the mid-19th century. Dorton was, and still remains a hamlet, by the Dorton estate with its large red brick Jacobean mansion.

In the early 1830's, news of the curative powers of the spring waters and the intended development of a spa at Dorton, to rival the best-known watering places, reached a wider public. Hitherto the local peasantry only had repaired thither for the healing water.

Mr. C. S. Ricketts who owned the Dorton estate, *'under the direction of a professional gentleman from London, James Hakewill',* * erected a Pump-room and Baths, after the design of the Tower of the Winds at Athens with decorations from the Temple of Jupiter Stator at Rome. It was entered by a flight of steps and through a semi-circular portico supported by columns with Corinthian capitals. A dome rose above the centre and the ceiling was supported by pillars painted to resemble Sienna marble. Besides the Pump-room and eight baths, there was a reading-room, billiard-room and two ballrooms.

Twelve acres of the park was laid out as pleasure grounds, planted with evergreens and shrubs, and a serpentine lake included. In June 1834 nearby land was offered on building leases for 99 years. This commanded *'a panoramic view of nine counties, and some of the most beautiful scenery in England, for salubrity and amenity unequalled within a few minutes' walk of the Pump-room and Mineral Springs.'*

At this time a handbill was circulated advertising a Promenade Musicale. Admittance to the Pump-room and grounds was 3/- each person, which included a Public Breakfast and a Band. The normal charge for a warm fresh water bath was five shillings – cold 3/-, warm chalybeate 3/6d., and cold 2/-. Admittance to the Pump-room and Grounds and drinking the waters cost one shilling per person. Family and Season tickets were available at reduced prices.

In March 1836, the Dorton Rural Hotel was available for letting. It was situated 10 minutes' walk from the Spa and had a 200-acre farm attached.

---

*Architect and author of 'Elizabethan Architecture', which he dedicated to Mr. Ricketts.

'From the constant influx of visitors attending the Spa, the hotel would be found a very desirable situation for business.' The influx of visitors kept the hotel going, at any rate until 1843, when the local magistrates granted it a licence.

The following June the *'Bucks Gazette'* reported, *'at this far-famed retreat, alterations, various and important, have been made since last season. The pleasure grounds and lake have been enlarged, and a flight of steps erected to descend to the boats, which will be a pleasant addition to those fond of aquatic amusements'.* It concluded on an ominous note, *'Doubtless the complaints which were made last season respecting the roads, will be taken into consideration.'* Meanwhile, the Pump-room had been *'ornamented with the works of some first-rate artists.'* In 1837 a Grand Fete took place at the Spa, probably to mark the accession of Queen Victoria.

Bucks Archaeological Society

DORTON SPA

'The Mirror of Literature, Amusement and Instruction,' for the 31st August, 1839, featured Dorton Spa. It said, *'This fashionable spa, having risen to a great eminence in the estimation of medical men, vast numbers have received relief by drinking its waters of 'nature's own preparing'.*

DORTON SPA.

BRILL,

PROMENADE MUSICALE.

The Public are most respectfully informed, that
On Thursday next, the 14th instant, at One o'clock,
THERE WILL BE

A PROMENADE MUSICALE.

The admission to the Pump Room and Pleasure Grounds on this day will be 3*s*. each person, which will include

A *Public Breakfast.*

It is also intended to have an additional Band on the occasion, to the usual one which attends every Monday and Thursday.

August, 1834.

H. BRADFORD, PRINTER, THAME.

Sister Sale MBE

Springs of the purest water arise from almost every hill. The neighbouring villages have been attracted from time immemorial to a stream issuing from a small orifice; which marked its course by the destruction which it occasioned to vegetable life.

They called it '*Alum Well*', the taste of this salt being most apparent. The cattle were allowed free access and those which laboured under any disease recurred to its use spontaneously and rapidly recovered. Many cases of human suffering exhibited on its application the same successful results.

The almost impassable state of the country roads until recently, joined to the advanced age of the proprietor, rendered it impossible to take any steps respecting the spring. At length the influx of visitors became so great, owing to the recent cures and at the same time the injury done to the fences and herbage became so serious that it was judged advisable to restrain the peasantry who flocked thither, to one path; to enclose the well and to appoint a superintendent to distribute the water: by these precautions from 50 to 100 gallons of water a day have been supplied to various applicants.

Certainty of its healing properties, corroborated by professor Brande, '*the proprietor has taken measures for giving to the public every facility of access*'.

Mr. T. Knight, a surgeon from Brill, after studying the professor's analysis of the water concluded '*that there was no other known in this country that compared with the strength of this chalybeate; and that there was only one spa in Germany which contained vitriolated iron to such a degree. The atmosphere over the well gives the strongest evidence of the existence of gases. On a temporary closure of the well, a body of gas collects sufficient to black a silver spoon.*'

A depot was opened in London for the sale of the Dorton Spa water. The analysis was printed and remarkable cures were claimed in order to recommend the spa's efficacy in treating a score of human ills. Even cases of cancer, leprosy and total blindness were said to have benefited.

But all efforts to promote the spa were of no avail. By 1862 it was said that, '*the chalybeate has, of late years, been little sought after, invalids preferring more fashionable localities.*' Its isolated situation made it impossible to sustain its popularity; the sanguine expectations of the promoters and their vision of '*many a line of villas that would speedily grace the spot,*' were unfulfilled. Dorton Spa had failed.

AMONG THE articles shown at the Buckinghamshire Archaeological Society's exhibition at the Town Hall, Aylesbury, in July 1905 were pieces of silk from Aylesbury Silk Mills dated 1869. It is surprising that silk weaving was carried on in the town and surrounding places during the first half of the last century. Several factories were established by two brothers who had connections with the industry in Manchester.

The first silk mill was erected at nearby Tring in 1824 for Mr. William Kaye, a stockbroker of Tring Park. It was occupied by his brother who had retired from a similar business in Manchester. Their nephew, Robert Nixon, and a colleague, Richard Moscrop, visited Tring Silk Mill with a view to starting a similar business where cheap labour was plentiful. This they found at Aylesbury and nearby villages where unemployment was rife as the pillow lace making industry declined in competition with machine-made lace.

Aylesbury parish authorities gave assistance in establishing a new industry, and put up £200 towards the building on a part of old workhouse premises. In return Mr. Nixon agreed to employ only paupers chargeable to the parish. Forty looms were installed. Later the business was taken over by new employers who had succeeded to the Tring works. The Aylesbury premises were greatly enlarged.

This mill was solely for weaving the silk which was supplied partly from Tring. There were about seventy steam-power looms as well as hand-looms there. All classes of silk goods were produced, mostly in a finished state ready for the counters of the silk mercers. Aylesbury silk products were exported to Paris, re-imported to London and sold in the shops in the town as best French silk products.

At Whitchurch a few miles north of the town, *Messrs. Moscrop and Nixon* introduced silk weaving in 1838, placing a few looms in the cottages. Later others were set up in a building in the village and a small factory was started at Little London, which gave occupation to women and young girls. Mr.

Moscrop took up residence in the village and became known as *'Old Mossy'*. Finally, a new factory was erected which was dubbed appropriately *'Little Bolton'*. Here looms and machinery were installed with a warehouse and homes for employees. Articles were shown at the Great Exhibition of 1851. The factory employed about forty people who on average earned ten shillings a week. On Mr. Moscrop's death, the business declined.

A further branch of the Tring and Aylesbury concern was set up at Waddesdon in 1843, in a building which stood about the centre of the village, where many women were employed at hand-looms.

The introduction of silk weaving in mid-Buckinghamshire provided much needed work for the inhabitants at a time when employment was hard to find and relieved the local overseers of the poor of some of their financial burdens.

THE HALTON EXHIBITION 1868, AND 'MR. ALFRED'

THE HALTON Industrial Exhibition was opened by Benjamin Disraeli on June 1, 1868, and was held as *The Times* said, in *'one of the most secluded portions of the County of Buckingham'* – the Rothschild estate beneath the Chiltern Hills at Halton, now used by the Royal Air Force.

The exhibition *'originated in a desire on the part of members of the family of Sir Anthony de Rothschild to collect specimens of the industry of the residents in a single parish upon their estates'.* But pressure grew from nearby villages anxious to take part and finally fifty parishes entered.

There was straw plait made into bonnets, boxes and baskets; needlework, lace, silks and *'rugs made of fragments of cloth strung together';* all manner of things from ornamental glass and scientific models to bread freshly made and dairy butter; furniture and agricultural implements. In fact *'everything bearing on the daily lives of the people and their local industries especially where these gave indications of anything original or striking in character'.*

The model of a church made of 5,000 wine corks and 16,000 pins and the *'design for a mansion, the result of 20 years labour, made from fragments of chair legs and having a puzzle money-box on the first storey',* must have pleased the adjudicators chosen from *'persons of standing and reputation'* from outside the district.

Four acres of Halton park were devoted to *'wide saloons of canvas'* to accommodate 3,000 exhibitors. Lady de Rothschild invited local carpenters and builders to compete for prizes for model cottages, made to scale, *'in which greater attention was to be paid to substantial and interior comforts than to outward and architectural effects'.* Specifications and estimates were called for and the winner undertook to erect the cottage accordingly.

The band of the Grenadier Guards, reinforced by village school choirs, struck up *'A Song of Joyous Greeting'* as the distinguished guests assembled and Bucks Volunteers provided a guard of honour. Opening the exhibition, Mr. Disraeli touched upon *'the earnest movement to improve the residences of the working classes . . . uniting comfort and convenience with economy.'*

HALTON
Mr Disraeli opening the Industrial Exhibition

The *'marquee tastefully fitted up as a drawingroom with valuable paintings and furniture'* in a floral setting, intended for the Premier and Mrs. Disraeli, was scarcely used as the weather was so brilliant *'that to be out of doors was far preferable and in fact so great was the heat that it was impossible to remain under canvas'.*

There were 200 medals given as prizes, of which the Prime Minister said to laughter that one was certainly in gold; others of the sister, though less precious metal, and a considerable number of a more enduring material. Around 5,000 spectators paid 2s each on the first day. The exhibition lasted for a week. On the final days admission was reduced to 2d to enable all the local residents to attend.

In 1884, Mr. Alfred Charles de Rothschild erected Halton House. It was designed by Cubitt and built in a free French style, incorporating a grand central hall rising two storeys, decorated in white and gold. The staircase from the staircase hall had a bronze balustrade. Winter gardens were included in the scheme.

'Mr. Alfred', as he was known at Halton, was a colourful bachelor with sensitive features. He exercised a paternal lordship over his tenantry, who worked on the estate or served in the mansion where entertainment was especially lavish on royal occasions, such as the visit by the Shah of Persia and Prince Albert Victor in 1889.

Outside staff and estate workers occupied decorative houses and cottages having the Victorian Rothschild stamp upon them, being embellished with arms, monograms and plaster pictures depicting the four seasons, woodcutting and country crafts. Mr. Alfred encouraged such pursuits by an annual agricultural show. His private orchestra, which on occasions he personally conducted at the mansion, played while sightseers ambled round the marquees; awed by the size of the vegetables and enraptured by blooms from Halton hot-houses, alongside specimens from the under-gardeners' private plots.

Halton embraced everything that Mr. Alfred deemed beneficial for the welfare of his visitors and employees. High in the Chilterns he built a timber chalet in 1888. Here visitors could take the air and survey the Vale of Aylesbury. Skittles could be had in an adjacent alley and pekinese fondled in the breeding kennels.

In a field near the mansion Mr. Alfred's circus of animals performed. Mr. Alfred himself, attired in a frock coat with a whip and white gloves, took part as the ringmaster or drove visitors round in his zebra four-in-hand. Mr. Alfred's private train brought visitors from London. Eminent medical men were sometimes among them, possibly because Mr. Alfred, being a bachelor, had a bachelor's inclination to study his health. Visitors arrived from Tring station in one of his many motors painted blue picked out in yellow, which were the Rothschild racing colours.

Dotted among the woods of the estate were a cricket field with a pavilion, a horse-drawn fire-engine manned by eleven men, and a full scale laundry.

From Halton Woods in 1917, Mr. Alfred offered timber to make props for dug-outs on the Western Front. He died in January 1918.

Men from Kitchener's army were pitching tents on the estate. Mud and illness were rife. Tents gave way to huts when the Royal Flying Corps moved in. The huts were replaced by brick barracks. The first entry of aircraft apprentices arrived in January, 1922. The Rothschild image had faded. The Royal Air Force had taken over the estate and carried the name of Halton across the world.

MR ALFRED

FOUR MOTOR cars and their owners attended the first meeting of the Aylesbury and District Automobile Club on May 12, 1904. They assembled alongside nine motor-bicycles and a motor-tricycle in Kingsbury Square, Aylesbury, before driving to Oxford, and lined up near the Royal Bucks Hospital to be photographed.

Hayward Parrott

Among the cars was BH36, a dark green De Dion Bouton Voiturette of 4½ hp, and weight 7 cwt., licensed by the county council on December 10, 1903. This belonged to the writer's father, Dr. T. G. Parrott, and had tiller steering and two bench seats facing each other.

BH150 was a similar car which was owned by Mr. John Kingham of Kingham & Bowker's garage, High Street, Aylesbury. It was licensed on January 1, 1904.

BH245 was a dark green single Phaeton Swift of 5 hp and weight 5 cwt. It was licensed to Mr. Percy Young, of 10 Market Square, Aylesbury, on March 18, 1904.

BW175 was registered in Oxfordshire.

Another pioneer owner of the time was the then Earl of Buckinghamshire, who had a 10 hp single cylinder car made by the Argyll Company at Govan, Scotland, in 1903. Those in the photograph (from left to right) are the Earl, Mr. George Oakes, his valet, and at the wheel Mr. George Sadler, who, it is understood, owned a garage in Great Missenden. The fourth passenger is unknown. The Argyll boasted a blue and black tonneau body picked out with yellow, and weighed 14 cwt. It was registered on December 3, 1903, and numbered BH15.

Hayward Parrott

BH 15

A handsome fleet of motor cars belonged to Mr. Alfred de Rothschild, of Halton House. There were not less than six cars at Halton during the 1903–4 period, BH55, Wolseley 12 hp, 18 cwt., registered in December, 1903; BH426, Renault Brougham, 15–18 hp, weight 1 ton 7 cwt., and registered in December, 1904; BH1010, 4-cylinder Zedel Phaeton, painted blue, and with a 1910 engine; BH 955, another Renault; and BH56, Elswick 24 hp, weight 1 ton, registered December 1903.

Another of Mr. Alfred's vehicles was BH408, a blue Victoria car weighing about a ton and registered on October 18, 1904.

Other early motorists in the district were Mr. R. G. Thomas, the county surveyor, who owned a Vulcan, Dr. Baker, of Church Street, Aylesbury, started with a De Dion and changed to a T-model Ford (BH111). Mr. Birch Reynoldson boasted an Oldsmobile steam car, while Dr. Donald Stewart, of the Prebendal, Aylesbury, ran an Alldays & Onions.

Motorists or motor-cyclists included Mr. A. C. de Fraine, Mr. Eborn, who started work at Kingham and Bowker's garage and moved to Mr. T. Adkins' garage in High Street, Aylesbury, before starting his own business in Walton Street; and Mr. T. Adkins, who had also been at Kingham & Bowker's. Also Mr. Bishop, watchmaker, of Walton Street, Aylesbury; Mr. Biggs, of North Marston; Mr. A. T. Thorpe, who before his retirement owned a garage in Bourbon Street, Aylesbury; Mr. Ted Cannon, of Ward & Cannon, Aylesbury, builders; and Mr. F. H. Parrott, who had an Alldays & Onions, and later a bullnosed Morris Cowley, BH600.

Mr. Thorpe and Mr. Keen, another driver of the time, collected the first Vauxhall that came to Aylesbury. The first T-model Ford locally was bought by Dr. Leonard West, of Wendover, for £125 (the list price was reduced later to £100). It took three days to bring it from Manchester.

The first prosecution in the county under the Motor Car Act, 1903, was heard at Aylesbury on February 20, 1904. The charge of driving a motor car to the common danger in Aylesbury was dismissed, the defendant paying the costs.

The writer has been helped by first-hand knowledge of early drivers and their cars, given to him by the late Mr. A. E. Thorpe, who kindly loaned the photograph of the Earl of Buckinghamshire's car.

Hayward Parrott

BH 408

WHEN A Rothschild mansion was erected round about the Vale of Aylesbury, which happened on several occasions in the latter half of the 19th century, that was not the end of it as far as the mansion or the adjacent village was concerned.

The instalment of a member of the family on his estate, was preceded by the development of the village by building largish dwellings with characteristic ornamentation, to house the steward, estate and farm managers, the head gardener, together with entrance lodges and staff cottages. Later, as at Waddesdon, a village hall and a hotel were built by the main road through the village. The latter bears the sign of *'The Five Arrows'*, symbolising the five sons of Mayer Amschel Rothschild who founded the great Frankfurt banking house.

Baron Ferdinand de Rothschild built Waddesdon in the French Renaissance style. Work started about 1879, and the main part of the mansion was completed in 1883. Baron Ferdinand was a grandson of the founder of the Austrian line and married his English cousin, Evelina, daughter of Baron Lionel de Rothschild. Sadly she died in childbirth leaving the Baron to carry on by himself with his plans to build a home in Buckinghamshire.

In 1874 he had bought Lodge Hill and some 2,700 acres of land from the Duke of Marlborough. Lodge Hill, the site of the Manor, was then almost bare, having only a farmhouse reached by a cart track. The highest part of the eminence was lowered and a site levelled for the house. Water was brought to it from 14 miles away and a tramway laid down to convey the great quantities of building materials from Quainton station. Teams of Percheron mares dragged them up the hillside.

Hundreds of grown trees were uprooted, conveyed long distances and replanted at Waddesdon. Great chestnut trees from local sources were towed by sixteen strong horses for each tree, the telegraph lines having to be lowered to let them go by. Eventually with its shrubberies, lawns, flowerbeds, home farm, aviary, marble statues and vases, and fountains which set off the wonderful view which Baron Ferdinand had always admired, Waddesdon Manor settled down among its beautiful surroundings.

Soon the eminent of the land progressed to Waddesdon. In July 1883, King Edward VIIth, then Prince of Wales, journeyed by train to Aylesbury and thence to Waddesdon. Six years later the Shah of Persia and Prince Albert Victor (later Duke of Clarence) proceeded from Halton (Mr. Alfred de Rothschild's house) to Waddesdon. By 1890 all was ready for Queen Victoria

The Illustrated London News

WADDESDON
The arrival of Queen Victoria at the Manor

to spend a day there. Local school children watched her arrival from stands erected by the main gates. Her Majesty toured the grounds in a bath chair drawn by a pony.

Baron Ferdinand died at the age of 59 and was succeeded by his sister Miss Alice de Rothschild, who for many years had lived with him. Miss Alice, of somewhat sombre appearance had a reputation for knowing her own mind, mingled with kindness and concern for others. An old retainer once said of her, *'She was always very particular but also very fair'*. On one occasion Miss Alice is said to have remarked, *'No man will marry me for my looks so he's not going to marry me for my money'*. The writer remembers seeing her in Aylesbury alighting from her carriage. She was attired in a plain grey costume.

The village athletic sports were held on the cricket ground in the park and the Temperance Band played at local events which took place there. Once when presenting prizes for the best flower garden, Miss Alice said, *'Life is like a flower garden. We can make it beautiful or otherwise at our own will. Sad and unhappy people were often to blame for their own sadness and unhappiness, for they had not sown flowers in their lives. Those who sowed flowers in their gardens and in their lives would be happy.'*

Miss Alice de Rothschild died in 1922 leaving Waddesdon to her great-nephew, Mr. James de Rothschild, a grandson of the founder of the French branch of the family. During the last war he opened the house to accommodate a hundred children in a residential nursery. After his death in 1957, the property passed under his will to the National Trust for all to see and appreciate the great house, its beautiful grounds, the splendid views, and the great art collections.

THE CHILTERNS SCHOOL

THE REV. Charles Edmund Roberts, M.A., was for many years before the First World War and some time after, rector of Halton, Buckinghamshire. At the rectory at World's End, a mile from his church, on the Aylesbury to Wendover road, he ran for thirty or forty years the Chilterns preparatory school for boys. Some twenty-six boys between the ages of eight and fourteen boarded there while the writer was at the school from 1918 to 1920.

Mrs. Roberts was kindness itself. Small boys away from home found in her a confidante and friend who listened to their troubles. Matron, short and stocky, with bunches of keys, scissors and what-not chained to her belt, inspired no such confidence. She exuded discipline and expected obedience. Miss Pitney taught music as an extra subject, and carpentry was another extra subject.

The foundation stone of the main grey brick house is dated 1867. The adjacent building seems earlier and at one time may have been a farmhouse. The entrance lodge was pulled down some years ago. There lived Mr. Damon, the gardener, and his wife. He wore a green serge apron when helping in the house or dining room.

Behind the front door of the rectory was the hall, with a tiled floor. Mr. Roberts's study lay to the left, impressed on the mind by a heavy aroma of pipe smoke. His vast roll-top desk filled the bay window. Here he edited the school magazine, *'The Chilternian'*. In later years he thrust forward his greying head from his shoulders. His annual sermon delivered at evensong on Palm Sunday in St. Mary's Church, Aylesbury, was traditional and drew a large congregation.

Across the hall was the drawingroom, seldom entered by boys after their first visit with parents to view the school. Elsewhere was the boys' dining room, with its memory of tapioca pudding resembling frog spawn and tasting of cloves, served in enamel pie-dishes. The main classroom, corridors lined with clothes hooks, the washroom and the kitchen quarters were at the rear.

Upstairs were three dormitories, the '*kitchen*' dormitory for small boys being above that place. The blue and pink dormitories overlooked the lawns. At the rear of the playground was a small building which housed Mr. Roberts's museum of natural history and curios. There were stuffed fish caught from Halton reservoir. Over it was a bedroom for two boys, which the writer once shared with another Aylesbury boy who became headmaster of a public school.

The gymnasium had the usual parallel bars and was the scene of boxing and

Hayward Parrott

THE CHILTERNS SCHOOL
1919

bleeding noses. Beyond the vegetable garden each boy had his own garden plot to cultivate. Then came the playing field for football and sports. Puffballs, a fungus which emitted powder when broken, were found here. As a boy, the writer thought they emanated from passing railway engines.

In term little was seen of the outside world. Road transport was scarce. At that time the first Aylesbury to Wendover motor bus passed the school. It was run by Mr. Young of Aylesbury, had an open top deck and was painted maroon. On summer afternoons the boys bathed in the reservoir, from the muddy beach at the Weston Turville end, supervised by Mr. Davis or Mr. Lewis, two young masters. A garden fete in aid of Halton church funds was held on the lawns. Winter afternoons sent the boys running along the Nash Lee road collecting autumn-tinted foliage to draw and paint in class, taken by Mr. Fells from Aston Clinton.

On Sundays, each boy had to recite the catechism or the collect. Attendance at Halton church was rewarded by a coloured religious stamp to paste into an album with spaces for Sundays and church festivals. Going to church involved a mile walk by the path along the reservoir bank in dry weather, or if wet all the way by Halton Lane. The boys wore Eton jackets, stiff collars and black top-hats for this trek. Occasionally someone fainted during service.

Although the writer's relations lived only four miles away, visits to the school were made not more than once or twice a term. Days at home or half-term exeats were not allowed. The writer enjoyed acting as scorer when the cricket team played Christchurch choir school at Oxford. The teams had tea together in Christchurch Hall. The sports field of the Chilterns is now a nursery garden, so it is still a fruitful soil for growing things.

THE DINTON HERMIT

A FEW years ago all the local inhabitants had heard of the hermit at Dinton, near Aylesbury, even if they did not know that his name was John Bigg. A picture of Bigg adorns the inn sign of the Dinton Hermit at Ford village, one and a half miles from Dinton. A pair of his shoes survive; one of them was kept at Dinton Hall and the other was sent to the Ashmolean Museum, Oxford. This grotesque shoe was described by Thomas Hearne (1678–1735), the Oxford historian, in 1713, as *'vastly large, made up of about a thousand patches of leather'.*

John Bigg, believed to be a native of Dinton, was born or baptized on April 22, 1629, and was buried at Dinton on April 4, 1696. He was employed as a clerk by Simon Mayne the regicide (1612–61), who owned Dinton Hall. Mayne was related to many of the chief families that adopted the cause of Parliament. He was elected MP for Aylesbury and was one of the judges who signed Charles I's death warrant. In Buckinghamshire it was thought that Mayne's employee, John Bigg, was actually the king's executioner.

It was said that when living at Dinton Hall, Simon Mayne for a time eluded the Royalists by taking refuge in a secret hiding-place under the gables of the roof, to which he gained access by a tunnel lined with cloth. Three lower steps of a staircase lifted up to give entrance to the tunnel, through which he crawled up to his hidden chamber.

Simon Mayne yielded himself to the authorities in June 1660 and four months later stood his trial at the Old Bailey. After a poor defence, in which he pleaded illness and undue influence by others, he was found guilty and attainted. After committal to the Tower of London, his health deteriorated and he died there on April 13, 1661. His body was handed over to his widow for interment at Dinton church *'without ostentation'.*

Thomas Hearne's description of the Dinton hermit's behaviour and attire moved artists to portray this strange man. After the downfall of his master and the subsequent restoration of the royal line, John Bigg *'grew melancholy',* and

The Buces Collection

although having some means and being a fair scholar took himself to a cave in the grounds of Dinton Hall, where he lived the life of a hermit. His clothes consisted of trousers, coat and a hooded cloak which he kept going, like his shoes, by patching over patches. He existed on charity but never asked for anything but leather, which he pinned promptly on to his clothes or shoes at the most needed part. The shoes were composed of countless small patches of leather, in parts six to ten layers thick, fixed together with nails. Nothing of the original shoes could be seen except the remains of the inner sole. The Ashmolean shoe, measured on the bottom, was thirteen inches long and six inches across. In its dried state it weighed just over four pounds five ounces.

The hermit lived for about thirty-five years in the cave, which became known as Bigg's Cave. In summer he emerged and made his way in his unusual garb, frightening the children as he went, to the wooded slopes of the Chilterns at Kimble, five miles on foot from Dinton. In spite of his terrifying aspect and bad reputation, and probably prompted by curiosity, people came from all parts bringing the hermit food, ale and milk. He carried his liquid refreshments in three bottles, probably of leather, which were suspended from his waist and held strong beer, weak beer and milk respectively.

Sir John Vanhattem, who acquired Dinton Hall from a descendant of the regicide in 1727, had the ground at the site of Bigg's cave dug over, but nothing of interest was found. An etching of John Bigg was published in 1787 by Mr. W. Richardson *'at his Ancient and Modern Print Warehouse'* in the Strand, London. Today if anyone asks the way to the Dinton hermit he or she is probably seeking refreshment at the Dinton Hermit inn at the village of Ford.

THE REV. JOHN MASON OF WATER STRATFORD

FROM 1674 to 1694 Water Stratford* near Buckingham had as rector John Mason whose religious zeal ultimately became fanatical. He thought he was Elias and led the local country folk to believe in him.

Water Stratford seethed with religious fervour and wild ritual. The village was dubbed *Mount Zion.* Mason's followers sold their farms and cottages, collected their possessions and sheltered in barns near the rectory, to await the day of judgment, which Mason told them was on the way. They passed the days giving reign to their fervour by holding endless services which included wild dancing and hand-clapping, shrieking and singing to the sound of violins, tabours and pipes.

Mason hailed from a Northamptonshire clerical background. As a child his health was poor. He was sent to a school run by a local parson who foresaw that his pupil would grow into a violent zealot. In 1661 he became an undergraduate at Clare Hall, Cambridge, where he came under the influence of strong religious views in the university.

After taking his B.A. in 1664, he entered the church, became curate to a Northamptonshire rector and applied himself to study. In 1668, he returned to Cambridge for his M.A. and later that year became vicar of Stantonbury, near Stony Stratford, for six years. His parish was almost deserted. Services in the little church were infrequent. He was busy writing on theological and devotional matters most of which were published in his lifetime. While there he married and his wife bore him a daughter, Martha, in 1674.

In that year, the parishioners of Water Stratford gathered in their church for the institution of a new rector, the Rev. John Mason. The small Norman church of St. Giles which had been restored in 1652 had its nave and chancel further rebuilt in 1828. The north and south Norman doors have been preserved. The north chancel doorway depicts the Agnus Dei and has a dragon carved on the lintel, while the latter shows Christ in Majesty supported by two angels.

*It is not contended that Water Stratford lies within the Vale.

The rectory has been added to since John Mason's time. There John and Mary Mason had five other children baptised between 1677 and 1684. One of them, William, was Vicar of Mentmore, Bucks, from 1706 to 1744.

It was said that Mason was seldom free from violent pains in his head, and had delusions. He could not bear a noise and his sons read to him in whispers. He even feared the sound of his own footsteps. At times, he couldn't say family prayers for fear of disturbing his brain with the sound of his voice.

He was often enveloped in clouds of smoke, and this *'overheated his brain and kindled that zeal which wrought itself into new light and prophecy'.* At services *'his prayers were vehement. An awful silence between each petition doubled their length with a sort of divine breathings'.* His sermons were *'so earnest as not to leave a dry thread about him, and so long as to be always ready to faint before he gave over'.*

In 1687 Mason lost his wife and *'never rightly enjoyed himself'* after her death. His sister-in-law, Mrs. Holmes, came to keep house for the rector and his children.

By 1691, his health had begun to fail. He dwelt on the approaching second Advent. His followers, convinced of the imminent coming of the Lord, rapidly grew, whole families moved to Water Stratford, having done with wordly affairs. Several hundred people settled there. The rectory was packed. Others *'lay in the town and made themselves open partitions in the barn'.*

The crisis came on the First Sunday after Easter 1694. Mason had fasted through the Easter Services. In the small hours of the 16th April, he said *'on a sudden he had an Appearance of Jesus Christ to him in a deep scarlet robe to His feet, far surpassing anything in nature; His countenance was most comely and Majestik; Majesty enough to strike Terror into 10,000 blasphemers, and yet pleasant to behold'.*

The next day he recalled that *'the crimson or purple robe seemed to be dipped in the blood of His enemies'* and that he *'saw Christ sitting in a chair, and a candle lighted in a candlestick . . . he said many things but spoke no word – 'What need was there of saying anything when He has actually begun his reign – For His majestick looks said that he came to judge and condemn the greatest part of the world; and his smiling countenance said He would save Sion and the Holy Ground; that is, Water Stratford and its borders, and that he himself was neither in a dream, nor mad, nor drunken, neither was he affrighted.'*

News of the vision spread. Crowds gathered at the rectory to hear their prophet expound from an upper window. To fellow clergy he was reticent, but he preached twice daily to his people as long as he was able. Dr. Paxton of Buckingham saw no hope of Mason's recovering his health.

The prophet claimed that the Saviour conversed daily with him. His followers confirmed that *'this John was the true Elias, or harbinger of the Second Coming'*. *'The kingdom being already come,'* Mason ceased giving the Sacraments and praying because *'nothing remained to be prayed for'*.

The Water Stratford disciples became completely out of hand and indulged in orgies in the vast kitchen of the rectory. They danced and skipped night and day, screaming and clapping like maniacs; singing doggerel hymns to ballad tunes, accompanied by fiddlers, pipers, and singing boys; they cried *'Fire!'* as a warning of the pending destruction of the world.

Mrs. Holmes told a cousin, who hastened to Water Stratford and suggested bleeding the patient to dispense the vapours. But those in the rector's circle insisted that the elect would be gathered from all the world to the *Holy Ground* or *Hill of Zion* at Water Stratford, that was the close at the rear of the rectory. Pious people who had not heard of Water Stratford would be hauled there without their consent, by angels. They continued to watch for the Saviour by day and night.

Whit Sunday was expected to be the Coming, but the Reverend John Mason did not live to see it. He was buried at Water Stratford on 22nd May, 1694. No memorial was erected. After Whit Sunday most of the disciples stayed together saying that their call was yet to come and continued to pray and sing. They stocked up with provisions and remained in the rectory and barn until November, holding meetings on the Holy Ground.

It was rumoured that Mason would rise again from his tomb. To quell this idea the new rector had the grave opened in view of the followers. They were still unconvinced, some claimed that they had seen and spoken to Mason since his death. After eviction from the rectory and the *Holy Ground* they led a communal life and worshipped ecstatically for about twelve years, traces of the sect being found up to 1740.

For many years afterwards a story was current in the village that the ghost of a former rector had to be *'laid'* at a bend in the river called *'Parson's Hole'*.

WATER STRATFORD
Norman Doorway showing, in the tympanum, Christ in majesty

THE CASE OF CORBET

GETTING ON for two centuries ago, a denizen of Tring, that one-time centre of the straw-plait trade in the western corner of Hertfordshire and within a stone's throw of the Buckinghamshire boundary, as a result of his criminal activities, met an inglorious end in the latter county. The man's name was Corbet and he earned his living ostensibly by sweeping chimneys and catching rats on the farms in the villages around the district. It was while he was working on Mr. Richard Holt's farm at Bierton, Buckinghamshire, that Corbet conceived the act of murder which was to perpetuate his name for some generations after he had paid the penalty of being hung from the gallows that were erected near the scene of his misconceived killing.

While farmer Holt's daughter, Mary, lay fresh in her grave, Corbet watched through a window the pious man who was engaged in prayer. When night fell, the bereaved father went to bed. Corbet, who had lain in wait, stood his ladder against the chimney-stack and, reversing his usual mode of operation, climbed down the chimney into his victim's bedroom, and barbarously murdered the unhappy man in his troubled slumber. Collecting such booty as he could carry, Corbet left the farmhouse by the front door, but failed to notice that his dog, which had been waiting outside, had slipped inside the farmhouse, where he accidentally shut it in.

When the milk boy went to the house next morning and found that Holt was not up he called the neighbours, who discovered Corbet's dog in the house and the body of Mr. Richard Holt. The rat-catcher had fallen into his own trap. *'Guided by the dog, who followed the scent of his master'*, it is recorded, *'the constable succeeded in apprehending Corbet at Tring, with some of the stolen property in his possession.'* At his trial he was convicted and condemned to the gallows and to be hung on the gibbet.

But for the inhabitants of Bierton, this was not by any means the end of their acquaintance with Corbet. For nearly a century they were to be reminded of the grim event each time they passed the gibbet site on their daily errands.

In 1773 crowds of country folk assembled to witness the execution. The wooden frame which was used first as a gallows was some eighteen feet high. When the cart which had taken the murderer to the drop was drawn from under him and life pronounced extinct, the body was encased in irons and suspended, so that *'Mary Lane, who lived servant at the farmhouse adjoining, could see as she sat up in her bed the body of the murderer hanging from the gibbet; and the farmers who live higher up the village said that their parents were unable to open their windows until after the following harvest'.*

In 1774 a sporting character passing through the village offered an old shepherd half-a-crown to climb the post and draw a pair of black gloves over the hands of Corbet, and to hang a black scarf over his face, a feat which the shepherd successfully accomplished.

Twenty-two years after the execution of Corbet his skull was still on the gibbet, and it stayed there until the irons disintegrated and were lost. The remainder of the gibbet post was used as a gatepost and served that purpose until 1860, when it was taken down and bought by a shrewd craftsman who intended carving it into small fancy articles as sourvenirs. The hanging of Corbet was the last time the gibbet was used in Buckinghamshire.

JOHN WESTCAR OF CRESLOW

JOHN WESTCAR, the renowned grazier, occupied Creslow Manor and farmed the rich Creslow pastures from 1779 until his death in 1833. Creslow Manor, one of the most interesting medieval houses in Buckinghamshire, lies near Whitchurch, six miles from Aylesbury. Built of local limestone, the oldest parts date from about 1330. It has an octagonal tower with walls six feet thick, a great hall, a small crypt and the remains of the ancient parish church, which is now used for secular purposes. At the dissolution of the monasteries, Creslow, which had been held by the Knights Hospitallers, passed to the Crown but was later relinquished.

Creslow contained the largest field in the county, the *Great Ground or Pasture*, being over 300 acres in area. The farmland that comprises the whole of the ancient parish of Creslow covers between 800 and 900 acres. The pastures have long been noted for the quality of the fat cattle and sheep grazed on them. The richness of the grass is attributed to the underlying *Kimmeridge* clay. By a deed of Queen Elizabeth I they were placed under the chief officer of her kitchen for the benefit of her royal household, and the Crown installed a keeper of the manor house and pastures.

When Mr. Westcar, who came from Souldern in north Oxfordshire, took Creslow, he would have done so in the knowledge that there he would be able to fatten beasts and sheep worthy of the royal tradition.

When he was established at Creslow, he travelled to Gloucestershire, Herefordshire and elsewhere in the west, where he bought Hereford bullocks five or six years old which had been worked on the land. These bullocks were shod with *'flakes'*, flat curved pieces of iron about two and a half inches long, one on each *'claw'* of their feet. These were very necessary when they were employed as beasts of burden on rural roads. Mr. Westcar had the animals brought by road to Creslow, where he fattened them for market.

In 1798 the *Smithfield Cattle and Sheep Society* was founded, John Westcar being one of the founders. The first Smithfield fat stock show was held in a livery stable at Dolphin Yard, Smithfield, in December 1799. Prizes were offered in four classes for the best beast and best sheep fed on grass, hay, turnips, or cabbages; and for the best beast and best sheep fed on corn or oil cake. Mr. Westcar gained a prize with his fat ox, the weight and size of which were judged so remarkable that it sold for £100, an unusual sum in those days. It stood 6ft. 7in. high and weighed 241 stone.

This ox had been transported to London by canal boat from the wharf at Wendover to Blackfriars. The journey took two days and the animal was said to have *'lost no flesh from the easy way it travelled'*. Its owner was one of the first to use canal boats for sending fat cattle to the London markets instead of by road. In the next twelve years, Mr. Westcar sold twenty oxen for an average price in excess of £100 apiece, and he gained forty-two prizes at the Smithfield show between 1799 and 1821.

That John Westcar remembered the loyal service of his farm servants is shown by a memorial tablet which he had placed on the exterior wall at the south-west corner of the church at Whitchurch, as a just tribute to the memory of Thomas Sirett, who was a faithful and diligent servant to him at Creslow for more than thirty years. Thomas Sirett was killed on April 25, 1811, while driving a cow through a gateway, in his master's presence. He was sixty and is interred nearby. The memorial inscription concludes: *'May this record of his merits invite others to an imitation of his praiseworthy conduct.'*

John Westcar himself was killed by a fall from his pony in the *Great Pasture* at Creslow on April 24, 1833, at the age of eighty-four. A clump of trees was planted to mark the spot, which became known to later generations as *'the old man's clump'*. In the church at Whitchurch there is a white marble mural tablet to his memory. This depicts the famous grazier standing in front of a fat ox, with some sheep at his feet. This unusual and fine memorial was executed in bas-relief by the eminent British sculptor, John Gibson, R. A. (1790–1866), who worked in Rome. Gibson once said: *'The human figure concealed under a frock coat and trousers is not a fit subject for sculpture. I would rather avoid contemplating such objects'*.* For this reason John Westcar is depicted attired in a Roman toga. Gibson's ideas of what constituted suitable wearing apparel for his subjects, were not readily accepted by popular opinion at the time. The tablet also commemorates Mary Westcar, the grazier's wife, who died on March 15, 1781, at the early age of twenty-three, and ends with a quotation from Pope's Windsor Forest:

'Unblemished let me live, or die unknown:
Oh, grant an honest fame, or grant me none.'

---

*Dictionary of National Biography

The Bucks Collection

CRESLOW MANOR

John Westcar of Creslow Manor was one of the outstanding farmers of his day. He was a country gentleman of taste and culture. A box pew was retained for his use in the church at Whitchurch. The fact that so noted a sculptor as John Gibson was commissioned to carve his memorial shows that he was also a gentleman of means. By his will he left £500 each to the parishes of Whitchurch and Cublington in Buckinghamshire and the parish of Souldern in Oxfordshire, whence he had come, for the benefit of the poor. The famous grazier was laid to rest at Whitchurch on May Day, 1833. He had no son, so his nephew, Richard Rowland, succeeded him in the tenancy of Creslow.

NORTH MARSTON MISER

ONE BITTERLY cold day in the last century a stage-coach stopped at an inn in a country town. The outside passengers, in greatcoats, climbed down and closed round the parlour fire, quaffing brandy to warm themselves. A shabby man without an overcoat kept his seat on the back of the coach. Sorry for the poor chap, his fellow travellers had a whip round and took him out a glass of spirit, which he drained gratefully. The *'poor chap'* was John Camden Neild, a barrister who owned property at North Marston, Buckinghamshire. He lived at Cheyne Walk, Chelsea, and died in 1852 leaving an estate worth £250,000.

Neild was born in 1780. His father, James Neild, a prosperous London goldsmith and pioneer of prison reform, sent his son to Cambridge and saw him called to the Bar in 1808. On his father's death in 1814, John Camden Neild came into property valued at £250,000. He did not, however, inherit his father's benevolent and reforming ways, for John Camden Neild became an eccentric miser.

Fate decreed that he was ugly, being short and stocky with a large round head set on a short neck. He wore a shabby blue swallow-tailed coat with gilt buttons, brown trousers, gaiters, and down-at-heel shoes. His clothes were never brushed because it might destroy the nap and wear them out faster. His London house, where he lived with a housekeeper, a maidservant and a favourite black cat, was scantily furnished. Here he slept on a bare board, but ended his days on an old stump bedstead.

He paid regular visits to the home counties collecting rents and staying the night with his tenants. His scattered estates entailed long journeys on foot. His only protection from the weather was an old green cotton umbrella, as he thought a greatcoat a needless luxury. He was often seen perched on a wagon of coal or huddled in a dirty farm cart if it was going his way. The driver received a penny or two for the lift, as Neild disliked receiving something without token payment.

When he was forty-eight, he tried to commit suicide at a farm at North Marston. His life was saved by the prompt action of Mrs. Neale, his tenant's wife. This rash act was due to a fall in the price of investments he had bought. The same lady, daughter of a former rector of the parish, used to darn Neild's underwear and stockings when he had gone to bed. Early next morning he gave her two pence to boil him two eggs, which he ate with a penny roll as he walked six miles into Aylesbury to get the London coach. At the county town, he called at the White Hart hotel and ordered cold beef for lunch. Once the waiter went unexpectedly into the room and found Neild had made a mighty beef sandwich and pocketed it, to save himself buying a dinner later. He was charged a shilling for it and grudgingly paid up.

In happier mood Neild once gave a pound to the Sunday school at North Marston and a few pounds to another school building fund; he sent £50 to a

NORTH MARSTON CHURCH, BUCKS, S.

Sister Sale MBE

G. C. & M. Farnell

NORTH MARSTON
View of the Church showing Queen Victoria's window

training college and supported the London Asylum for the Blind and the Buckinghamshire Infirmary. At times he probably assisted paupers if convinced of their need. It was largely through his advice and help that the boy Henry Tattam, a farmer's son at North Marston, entered university and took holy orders. Tattam studied Greek while he milked his father's cows, by hanging a book from a cord with a counterweight at the other end which was flung over the cow's back. In 1844, as Dr. Tattam, an Oriental scholar and rector of St. Cuthbert's, Bedford, he was appointed archdeacon of Bedford.

John Camden Neild died at Cheyne Walk on August 30, 1852, aged seventy-two. His favourite black cat was in the room. The funeral procession from Chelsea provided a spectacle for the crowds gathered by the way as it rumbled over the dusty roads of Buckinghamshire. It contrasted strangely with the dead man's lifetime mode of travel. At North Marston the church was packed with sightseers, who murmured, *'Poor creature! Had he known so much would be spent on his funeral he would have come here to die, to save the expense!'* The remains of this lonely man were interred beneath the chancel floor, where an engraved tablet marks the spot.

When his will was proved it caused a sensation. After a few small legacies the whole of his personal estate, sworn at *'under £250,000'* was left to Queen Victoria. The Keeper of her Majesty's Privy Purse, Archdeacon Tattam and one other were executors. The queen graciously increased their legacies from £100 to £1,000 each; provided for Mr. Neild's old housekeeper, as after twenty-six years' service he had omitted to do so; and bought an annuity for Mrs. Neale who had thwarted the testator's attempted suicide.

In 1855 the Queen restored the chancel of North Marston church, the roof of which John Camden Neild, as lessee of the rectory, had once repaired with strips of painted calico, saying *'they will last my time'*. She also installed an east window of stained glass and a sculptured reredos of Caen stone in memory of her unexpected benefactor.

If you come across a *'poor chap'* down on his luck, of your charity have a whip round for him!

HAPPY IS the town adult who harbours memories of childhood holidays spent on a farm, or of longer stays through wartime evacuation of children. Down on the farm timeless hours were passed playing in the old barn, or lying among the scented hay with a book. The sense of having eluded the grown-ups and found a solitary haven or joined with other children in a secret picnic when cordials swilled straight from the bottle tasted all the sweeter, became an indelible memory.

The word *'barn'* is derived from two Old English words *'bere-ern'*, meaning barley-house. Barns for the housing of livestock, storage of hay, straw, and other crops, farm wagons and implements, go back many centuries. Where stone was quarried locally, it was sometimes used for such purposes. Large barns often had a roof constructed of open timber framing. Spacious barns such as these might be divided into nave and side aisles as in churches. Old country barns often show on their exterior walls their timber-framed construction, infilled with brick nogging. Originally such infilling may have been wattle and daub. Nearly all old barns were entirely closed in and many originally had thatched roofs.

The Bucks Collection

WADDESDON
Thatched barn

G. C. & M. Farnell

TERRICK
Interior of timber barn

Barns have always served a number of incidental uses. Tithe barns were used for storing grain paid to the church as a tenth part of a farmer's yield from his crops. Others from time back afforded shelter to the traveller looking for somewhere to lay his head. In wartime or on military manoeuvres soldiers on the march have been billeted within their friendly walls. In past times, they were the focal point of the harvest supper when the crops being safely gathered, the farmer and his family presided over a scene of jollity and warmth which has never been surpassed in the annals of rural customs.

Some barns have through association with eminent persons, great size or remarkable construction, become known and merit a visit. One of these is the big barn at Old Jordans Farm where Quakers held their meetings at least as early as 1669 before the famous meeting-house was built further down the road. It is thought that the big barn could have been built with timbers taken from the *Mayflower* in which the Pilgrim Fathers sailed from Plymouth to America in 1620.

For many years now Dutch barns have become a part of the British farm scene. Constructed of strong stanchions holding up galvanized iron or light metal roofs, with one or more sides open to the weather, the cost of building is more economical. Will they foster happy memories for children down on the farm, as did the old-time barn?

SOME OLD BREWERIES

IN THE last half of Queen Victoria's reign and the first part of the present century every small town had at least one brewery. Before that many inns brewed their own ale on the premises. Thus in 1843 Thomas Wootton, of the Bear in Walton Street, Aylesbury, intimated that he had extended his brewing department and could supply families with genuine home-brewed beer. Good fresh table beer was threepence per gallon and good ale tenpence per gallon, delivered in the town for ready money.

In the 1850s Alfred Barton, of the George inn, Winslow, was also a maltster, brewer and dealer in hops, as was George Webb, of Market Hill, Buckingham. William Hipwell, of the Bull Hotel, Olney, brewed *'choice Olney ale and porter'*. The Wendover brewery belonged to Joseph Holland of the Red Lion Hotel there.

From these origins grew local breweries which in time swallowed up smaller rivals or put them out of business and later formed public companies, firms which have been absorbed themselves by larger concerns or a fair stake of whose equity is held by them. Thus the big groups came into being. Fairly few small towns still have a working brewery.

Old directories carry many small brewers' advertisements. In Aylesbury in the 1890's there was C. K. Thomas, of Castle Street. The manager was John Hamblen, who filled farmers' own casks. By 1913 he had acquired the business and offered invalid stout at 1/3d and 1/6d per gallon. The firm was taken over by Gullivers, of Aylesbury. Brewing ceased during or soon after World War I.

In the 1850's, among others, Edward Terry brewed in Walton, Aylesbury, and John Dell brewed in Bourbon Street, which was once called *Waterhouse Street* from the waterhouse connected with the brewery. By the latter part of the century Dell's brewery was trading as Messrs. J. and T. Parrott, which later became part of Messrs. Parrott, Walker and Company of the Walton brewery, Aylesbury, which itself was acquired by the Aylesbury Brewery Company Ltd. The company was registered in 1895. A year later it took over

Hayward Parrott

ROWSHAM
Old brewery

Frank Higgens and Company Ltd., of the Swan Brewery, Buckingham, and in 1899 acquired the Bletchley Brewery Company Ltd.

Thomas Parson ran the Lion Brewery at Princes Risborough in the 1880s and 1890s. This was acquired by the Aylesbury Brewery Company about 1920. A few years ago an ornamental lion stood near the entrance to the old premises in the market place.

At the turn of the century H. J. Barber and Company were brewing at Aston Clinton (formerly Mr. John Sheerman's brewery). It was claimed that the spring water used was equal in quality to that at Burton. Local barley and Kent and Farnham hops were used. The price list included *Barclay Perkins stout at 54/- per barrel, pale ale and porter at 35/- and bottled ale at 2/6d per dozen.*

At Ivinghoe in the 1880s onwards there was Messrs. Roberts and Wilson's brewery. Their trade mark was a horseshoe. It was acquired by Benskin's Watford Brewery in 1927. The brewer's house is now used as a Youth Hostel.

IVINGHOE
Messrs Roberts and Wilson's Brewery and House

G. C. & M. Farnell

ROWSHAM
Malt house

Rowsham, beyond Bierton, Aylesbury, had its brewery. At one time it traded as Lucas and Lovett but was owned mainly by the old local family of Lucas. Mr. Joseph Lucas, brewer and grazier, who died in 1832, built himself a handsome residence at Rowsham. Mr. Thomas Gurney was the last to brew there. Operations ceased some time after 1939. Part of the premises has now been converted to a private house.

Chesham had William Darvell's brewery in High Street. He claimed the invention of an improved refrigerator, which he exhibited at the Great Exhibition in 1851 and which he found a considerable saving and advantage over the old cooling system. The Chesham brewery was acquired by Taylor, Walker and Company Ltd. in 1956 and closed in 1957.

In the old times brands of beer were legion and everyone could choose the inn or brewery that pleased his palate. Against the departure of local labels must be seen the superior amenities and services rendered by brewery companies and licensed houses to their present patrons.

SOME OLD BRIDGES

OLD BRIDGES disappear in rising numbers as modern traffic renders them too narrow and unable to bear present loads. So many have been demolished to make way for new ones on the same sites that structures dating back several hundred years are uncommon.

G. C. & M. Farnell

THORNBOROUGH

The medieval bridge. Beyond, to the right, can be seen two Roman tumulii

The only medieval bridge in Buckinghamshire remains at Thornborough on the Buckingham to Bletchley road. It has three-pointed ribbed arches, and two plain ones to the east, and three breakwaters on the south side. A plaque thereon states that it *'was repaired at the charge of the County Ano Dominy 166(?) according to a Sessions Order. Sr. Richard Temple Sr. Toby Tyrel Barronets and Thomas Stafford Esqre being appointed to take Order for the doing of the same and William Woollhead of Thornborow ye (?) of the said work'*. Two shields show that Thomas Ward and Robert Collison were the *'Masuns'* employed on the work. Nearby, the site of the Roman crossing has been uncovered and can be seen. The old bridge took only one line of traffic.

Old Hardwick bridge over the Creslow brook on the Aylesbury to Buckingham road was widened a few years ago and lost its stone parapets. The old bridge was built in 1839 at the expense of the trustees of the Wendover to Buckingham turnpike road and the county, thereafter becoming a county bridge. It was itself a replacement of an earlier one. The old ford alongside is there still.

G. C. & M. Farnell

WINSLOW BRIDGE

Brick built bridges carrying secondary roads over rivulets have their charm, such as that on the Aylesbury road just south of Winslow bridging a tributary of the River Ouse. The main road has been diverted so that the old bridge now forms part of a layby among fine trees.

In olden times the repair of bridges was in some places considered of almost equal importance as the repair of churches, the duties of supervising repairs and upkeep sometimes being vested in the same bodies. Grants of money and bequests might be made for a parish church and a nearby bridge.

THE STREETS of country towns and village lanes in Buckinghamshire harbour a remarkable array of building styles in non-conformist places of worship, from the humble converted cottage to the formal Italianate town edifice reminiscent of a child's box of coloured building bricks. Usually not so prominent a feature as the parish church they have however a definite niche in the community scene.

Such buildings erected earlier than the 18th century seem to be rare. One is the Quaker Meeting House at Jordans, Buckinghamshire, which was erected in 1688 and includes a home for the caretaker. Prior to that the Friends held meetings at nearby Old Jordans Farm and The Grange, Chalfont St. Giles. The simple gravestones of William Penn and his two wives and his friends Isaac

Hayward Parrott

WADDESDON HILL BAPTIST CHAPEL

Hayward Parrott

WESTON TURVILLE
The Union Chapel

Penington and Thomas Ellwood are at Jordans.

Keach's Baptist Chapel near Winslow market yard bears the date 1695. The late Georgian furnishings are complete. Some years ago the chapel was restored with the aid of a grant from the Historic Churches Trust. This chapel has links with Benjamin Keach (1640–1704). From the age of nineteen, he was a zealous Baptist preacher, born at Stoke Hammond and baptised in the parish church. Through John Russell, a Baptist minister at Chesham, he was baptised again at fifteen and worked as a tailor. In 1664 he was seized and imprisoned for preaching at Winslow, where he met his wife, Jane Grove, and ministered in the chapel in Pillar's Ditch. Later he was tried at Aylesbury for writing the *'Child's Instructor'*, a catechism, sent to prison without bail and sentenced to stand in the pillory there in the market place, and also at Winslow, where his *'seditious and venomous book'* was burnt before his face. Some time later after preaching at Winslow he was seized violently from the meeting house, tied across a horse and taken to Aylesbury for further trial.

Another early Baptist Chapel of interest is at the top of Waddesdon Hill on the way to Upper Winchendon. It was built in 1792 at the expense of Mr. Francis Cox, who died in 1803 and was buried in the chapel. Outside the wall is a stone horse-mounting block.

The Union Chapel at Weston Turville has a neat homely aspect and was erected in 1839 with later extension. Possibly a bit earlier is the humble Congregational Church at Great Horwood with its pointed windows and portico at the side.

With a simple classic form in brick, the Tabernacle Baptist Chapel and Centenary Hall at Winslow was built in 1864. It is tucked away down a passage off the main road to Buckingham. A few years later, in 1882, the former Primitive Methodist Chapel in Buckingham Street, Aylesbury, was put up. A picture of it almost moves one to find a box of building bricks and make a model of it. It was knocked down a few years ago.

Unusual was the boatmen's chapel which prior to the early 1920s stood by Aylesbury canal basin. Sunday services were held for bargemen and their families. The roof resembled an old barge turned upside down.

This short article may be a reminder that many old non-conformist chapels and meeting houses have much of interest which is often overlooked.

COMPARATIVELY FEW gravestones were erected in churchyards prior to the 17th century. Many interments took place inside the church itself and were marked by slabs of stone or slate known as ledgers, set in the floor, sometimes with added brass likenesses of those laid to rest. Statesmen, the nation's eminent men, and wealthy estate owners often furnished chapels and hired skilled sculptors to fashion magnificent altar tombs and wall monuments to their memory.

From the 17th century onwards, gravestones started to thicken in churchyards, owing to various factors. Space within the church was limited, the populace was increasing and perhaps money itself had a bearing on the matter. Farmers and tradesmen could now afford to erect a stone on the greensward.

Slowly the south side of the churchyard became filled, this position being preferred. The north side of the church, associated with the devil, was used to bury those of ill repute or those who had died unbaptised. Consequently the oldest stones, usually rather stunted and thick, are mainly on the south side.

G. C. & M. Farnell

ICKFORD
Churchyard gravestones

Hayward Parrott

AYLESBURY

Memorial denoting that the family line has died out

Hayward Parrott

HARTWELL

Stone needle marks the opening of the Churchyard; May 1756

Altar and table tombs are to be found, as are ledger stones and the long succession of headstones with all manner of carved inscriptions, from the melancholy to the humorous and witty. Angels and cherubs, hour glasses and scythes, all symbols of mortality, are frequent. Sometimes a flat or rounded stone is placed horizontally between head and foot stones, representing a body.

Upright iron memorials were also used in some localities, with ornate railings. For economy wooden grave boards were used in the 18th and 19th centuries, but by their nature few survive in good condition.

Only late in the last century was white marble imported in quantity from Italy, and sometimes a polished black marble slab is also encountered, but such memorials are not of the old English churchyard tradition.

Occasionally a memorial of unusual significance is found in a churchyard; such things being mistaken for family memorials until their inscriptions are read. One such is at Hartwell churchyard, near Aylesbury, where a stone needle marks the date when the churchyard was opened in May 1756.

Ellesborough churchyard, high on a spur of the Chilterns, falls away steeply on all sides of the church. Facing the path leading to the south porch is a stone calvary dedicated to all those interred in the churchyard. It was erected in 1897.

A memorial with a broken column which is sometimes seen; the head of the column rests on the ground below; signifies that the family line has died out.

With shortage of labour and rising maintenance costs, many churchyards have become sadly neglected. In some of them the old headstones have been taken up and replaced in rows by the churchyard walls. This seems a better solution to the problem of upkeep than laying them horizontally to make footpaths, as has been done in a few places, to the detriment of the old inscriptions. For those so inclined a wander round an old village churchyard is not without its reward.

Hayward Parrott

NETHER WINCHENDON
Old wooden grave-board

VILLAGE CROSSES

YOUR VILLAGE or nearby town may have an old stone village market or churchyard cross, although the base with or without part of the shaft may be all that remains. Unrecognized by many, these bases lie grass-hidden in old churchyards. At Wing, Buckinghamshire, a sundial has been placed on the headless shaft. Villagers gathered round these crosses to learn of local or national events. In churchyards they were also places of devotion. Villagers knelt by the cross and offered a prayer before going to church. On occasions the priest addressed his flock from its steps.

Apart from memorial crosses to the dead, churchyard crosses were the earliest stationary crosses used in Britain. Christian missionaries erected crosses to mark the customary places of instruction in the faith. These sites might be surrounded by a bank or ditch to form an open-air sanctuary. Churches were sometimes built afterwards within the enclosures, which eventually became churchyards having their crosses, although both had existed before the church building. As the first wooden crosses decayed, they were replaced by stone ones, usually a single column mounted on a base formed of steps and surmounted by a cross.

Wayside crosses were erected from early times, often serving as boundary marks and guides to travellers. Transactions carried out in front of the town cross were considered binding and sacred. The earliest market and village crosses were plain, but later ornamentation was introduced. Some had shafts covered with interlaced patterns while the heads, especially of churchyard crosses, might be cross-shaped, having projecting niches to hold sacred figures such as Christ on the cross and the Virgin and Child. Others copied the elaborate Eleanor crosses which were erected at each place where in 1290 the body of Queen Eleanor had rested on the way from Nottinghamshire for burial in Westminster Abbey.

In larger towns and cities the early simple crosses often gave place to market or butter crosses, which themselves were sometimes replaced by

QUAINTON
Remains of the fifteenth century cross on the green

buildings containing a small room above a covered-in space under arches and buttresses. But it is the simple village cross on the green or in the churchyard, with its associations momentous and trivial to past generations, that is of lasting interest. If you have a cross or a part of one in your village it is worth a passing thought and preservation for the future.

Hayward Parrott

BOARSTALL
Here the ancient cross has been restored

Hayward Parrott

WING
A sundial has been added to the pillar of the ancient cross

ESTATE LODGES

A LODGE IS usually a small house in a private park or a gatekeeper's cottage, a dwelling subservient to the principal residence on a landed estate. Mansions surrounded by substantial acreage have often two or more such estate cottages placed by the main entrances to the property. They were built at such strategic points to make sure that someone was on the spot to open the gates to allow the equipage of the proprietor or his guest to proceed to or depart from the demesne.

Originally they probably served as the first line of defence of the owner's rights and privacy, and to some extent this may be true today. The gatehouse having rooms over the archway through which traffic passed appears to be inspired by the old castle gatehouses, which were primarily defensive in purpose. Lodges also provided useful homes for outdoor workers, who in old times numbered an army of craftsmen skilled in forestry, estate upkeep, agriculture and the care of horses for riding, driving, hunting and farming generally.

Nineteenth century landowners were at pains to provide their estate servants with housing, which needed to fit harmoniously into its surroundings and to provide suitable living quarters for the occupiers.

Architects of the period drew up countless designs for estate cottages, many of which took the form of lodges at park gates. Model plans were published by interested bodies. Typical of these activities in Buckinghamshire was a competition arranged by Lady de Rothschild in connection with the Halton Industrial Exhibition in 1868. She invited local carpenters and builders to compete for prizes for model cottages made to scale, in which *'greater attention was to be paid to substantial and interior comforts than to outward and architectural effects'*. Specifications and estimates were called for and the winner undertook to erect the cottage accordingly.

Lady de Rothschild's emphasis on interior comforts was far-seeing. Less enlightened proprietors tended to give priority to outward appearance and sometimes frivolous external decorations. In fact the de Rothschild families provided a wealth of park lodges and village houses on their Buckinghamshire estates at Waddesdon, Mentmore, Halton and elsewhere.

Numerous styles of lodges are found, but almost without exception, each is picturesque in its own right, forming a pleasant point of interest by the road. An unusual lodge is at the entrance to the drive from Beaconsfield at Hall Barn. Constructed of timber, its walls are covered with panels which supposedly formed Gothic bench ends, old wood panelling and bedheads. It struck the author of *Pevsner's Buckinghamshire edition*, which contains a picture of it, as *'gratifyingly gay and irresponsible'*.

Domestic quarters in the lodge were often restricted. There was not room to bring up a large family, but for an older couple without children and not fussy about amenities, they provided comfortable homes. What did the lone housewife think about having to leave her kitchen to run out into the rain and open the gate? Her husband might give an unwelcome visitor a sore ear – a chap who came to air his grievances concerning fences or ditches with the squire. As likely as not the squire would haul his keeper over the coals for

MENTMORE TOWERS
One of the lodges

G. C. & M. Farnell

MENTMORE TOWERS
The Main Gate Lodge

sending a neighbouring farmer on his way after he himself had requested the man to call to discuss a problem.

Where former landed estates situated on the fringes of the country towns have been split up and developed for housing, lodges and park cottages have sometimes become private dwellings, adapted to present day standards by their new owners.

FARM DWELLINGS throughout the country differ much in their styles of building. Unlike smaller cottage homes attached to smallholdings and compact modern houses erected since the Second World War, old farmhouses have one thing in common, that is plenty of space incorporated in solidly built houses intended to last.

These period houses were erected when young men and women from the villages looked naturally to the farmer for work on the farm or in his house. Little other employment was available apart from rural craft industries. This

J. Hawkins

ASTON ABBOTTS
Oxley's Farmhouse, Mr & Mrs William Elliott with four of their five children, 1870

may explain why farmhouses had so many rooms, to house not only the family but domestic and farm servants as well.

Keeping warm the living quarters of large houses was not then the problem or expense it is today. Wood and timber were at hand or easily obtainable for burning in open hearths. Large fires and broad chimneys spread warmth round the house, and bedrooms had fireplaces for use when needed.

The material of which old houses were constructed was dictated largely by what was available locally. In medieval times timber was used everywhere for buildings, at first of simple construction, the lower ends of the vertical posts resting on bases of stone. Later it became usual to support the posts on low bases built of stone or bricks. The spaces between the beams were filled in with wattle and daub, which gave way later to brick nogging.

By the 16th century more use was made of other materials such as granite, limestone, bricks made from local clay, and slates for roofing and cladding. The old stone houses in the Cotswolds come to mind. Some West Country farmhouses were built of cob, composed of clay with varying additives of ground chalk, slate and rubble plus some straw or hair to help it bind. This was built up step by step a few feet wide on a low wall of stone or brick, each stage being trodden down, covered with straw and left to dry and harden before the next stage was begun. It was weather-proof and durable.

Flint found a place in local building, sometimes employed with brickwork intervening. This is found in Norfolk, Sussex and round the Chiltern Hills. Granite was widely employed in Cornwall and elsewhere, local slates being used for roofing. A feature in some areas was the practice of tile-hanging the upper halves of walls for added protection against the weather. This was often the case in Kent and Sussex. Whereas in the south-eastern counties weather-boarding was the vogue, being painted white or tarred black according to local custom.

Villages and countryside would be bare and uninteresting without attractive old farmhouses, let alone the hospitable and cheerful folk who dwell in them.

ALTHOUGH RELEGATED to sporting and farming spheres the horse has left its mark on life in the motor age. Relics from periods when the horse was the chief means of motive power can be seen by the roadside and in towns and villages, eloquent memorials to a noble and industrious animal.

Old roads, unless modernised entirely, harbour souvenirs that were erected to guide the horse and his master. Milestones set up by trustees of turnpike roads are common. Earlier ones, being of stone, vary in shape along different trust roads. They gave the name of the place where located and the distances from the towns on the way, and the mileage to London was often added. In the early part of the nineteenth century cast-iron milestones were used too, as seen along the Aylesbury to Hockliffe Road.

Associated with the milestones are the toll-houses, little homes for the gate-keepers. The gates have long gone except where there is still a toll levied to cross a bridge over a river or to use a private road. The gate-keeper collected tolls from all drivers and mounted riders. The trustees often farmed the right to collect tolls to the highest bidder. The toll-houses have their main doors facing the road, as seen at Great Missenden, and elsewhere.

A few bridges erected by turnpike trustees survive on main roads. Some have been widened, but they become fewer every year. One is the stone bridge at Hardwick, near Aylesbury, on the A413 road. This was built in 1839 by the trustees of the Wendover to Buckingham turnpike trust alongside the ford across the Creslow brook. The ornamental trees planted at the time are there still. Occasionally an early pack-horse bridge can be found.

Essential for horse and rider were mounting blocks and drinking troughs along the road. Every inn had them near the stables in the yard or before the main entrance. A double-stepped block exists in the King's Head yard, Aylesbury. It serves as a stand for flower boxes. An old block used by the rural congregation remains at Waddesdon Hill chapel, west of Aylesbury. Many drinking troughs now act as flower beds by roadside inns, such as those at the

Black Horse and the Nag's Head, north and south of Great Missenden. Others were erected by public subscription, sometimes being memorials like that by the main road at Aston Clinton, to Louisa Lady de Rothschild.

The horse went to the village smithy, standing quietly while the blacksmith shod him. The passer-by whiffed the hot scent from the irons and heard the melody of hammer on anvil. The blacksmith's forge is now a rarity. The horseman went to the market town to find a saddler and harness maker,

Hayward Parrott

HALTON HOUSE

Mr Hubbard, agent to 'Mr Alfred', accompanied by a pony boy

who today is a craftsman hard to come by. Many shops that seem to be such are merely retailers of leather goods. One old saddler's shop belonged to a Mr. Boote, which sounds a suitable name.

Gaily painted inn signboards depict the loyal service of the horse in the recent past. There are over fifty signs that include the horse in the title. Inns named Three Horseshoes are common and were often placed after a long piece of road without any dwellings. Originally there may have been a forge adjacent. In recent years, a licensed house has been named the Horseless Carriage, a veteran car being the chief feature. So ends the story of the horse as a means of motive power.

BUCKINGHAMSHIRE VILLAGES, as elsewhere, have their share of interesting old inns, picturesque examples of different manners in domestic buildings put up over the centuries. The original structures have often been extended and sometimes refronted in later styles. Where this has been done windows and doorways of a later period will be noticed.

These haphazard *improvements* that have been carried out from time to time have resulted in the generous sprinkling of attractive old inns which beguile the visitor to the Vale of Aylesbury. They pop up in unexpected places, by the side of a country road with scarcely a house in view, or down a lane off a village green.

J. How

WENDOVER
The Two Brewers and the The White Swan adjoin in friendly rivalry

Some are sixteenth century thatched cottages with timber studding. Such places usually have low beams and inglenooks. Occasionally the weatherboarded house turns up, often in proximity to railway stations or halts. Then there is the double-fronted nineteenth century house with wide sash windows, or an old cottage which has had bay windows put in the ground floor to give more elbow room in the bar parlour.

In the Chilterns many houses are faced with flints picked off the fields. These contrast with red bricks round doors and windows. The Bat and Ball at Holmer Green is a good example. In the High Street at Wendover there are two houses that belong to the same brewery company. They are the Two Brewers and the White Swan, which adjoin each other in friendly rivalry.

Main-road inns have often been altered inside and out so as to present spurious *olde-worlde* features to the uncritical eyes; old inns that aim to attract cavalcades of motorists from London, necessitating huge car parks adjacent. The photograph shows two typical friendly little inns that grace our small towns and villages, the focal points where local dwellers can relax in each other's company. They have been improved within to meet modern needs and to please ladies who chose to accompany their men for a jolly evening. Some of the older *locals* do not always agree that such things are improvements. They prefer things much as they were when they were lads, with oak settle and a spitoon on the floor of the public bar.

William Shenstone, the eighteenth-century poet, wrote long ago:

Whoe'er has travelled life's dull round,
Where'er his stages may have been,
May sigh to think he still has found
The warmest welcome at an inn.

PARISH STOCKS

PUTTING A man in the stocks is an ancient punishment. Stocks are depicted in Anglo-Saxon documents, and a law of 1350 ordered their erection in all towns. In 1376, the Commons petitioned Edward III that villages might have them too. They were regularly used through the centuries, and many old stocks are still preserved, like those at Addington and Dinton, Buckinghamshire.

At Quainton the stocks were near to the old market cross on the green. One of the last occupants was an old and eccentric schoolmaster named Wheeler, one-time parish clerk. Unduly fond of drink, he was also the local scribe and poet. Another occupant was a tinker. After *'residence'* therein, he always claimed the stocks as his *'freehold'*, and never failed to visit them when passing through Quainton.

ADDINGTON
The village stocks

To be fixed in the stocks on market day, jostled by crowds making ribald remarks or twisting one's ears was not pleasant. This was the lot of those who over-filled their skins with alcohol, swore profusely, profaned Sunday, or spoiled for a fight.

In James I's reign, *'dead'* drunks could be fined 5/- or spend six hours in the stocks, whereas merely tippling incurred a fine of 4/- or four hours. In Charles II's time, indulging in sports and pastimes on Sunday was met by a fine of 3s. 4d. or three hours, and a 5/- fine or two hours for working on Sunday.

Parish constables had to see that the wooden posts and boards of the stocks were repaired. Omission to do this might lead to an appearance before the justices who could impose a fine. The common law allowed constables to put a man in the stocks for safe custody but not as a punishment, the latter being ordered only by the justices. Naturally, the constables used their powers broadly and did not always take offenders to court, although it was unusual for a constable to be charged with exceeding his authority.

In 1685, a complaint was presented to the court that John Law, petty constable of Marlow, had been *'malicious and vexatious in troubling his neighbours, under the pretence of his said office.'* It was proved that he *'did lately seiz and take into his custody out of the Crowne Inn in Great Marlow one John Oxlade, and did lay or sett in the stocks in the publique markett place att or about 8 of the clock at Night, tho it alsoe appeared to this Court that the said John Oxlade is a person of Civill life and conversation and att that time was not in any wise disorderly or abusive to any person, neither had he dranck one flaggon of beer'*. John Law lost his job.

In 1699, the stocks at Aylesbury were the subject of a complaint before the justices. A fellow justice stated that being *'placed under a mudd wall tyled that incloses the garden belonging to his Mansion and that by the help of the said stocks, persons may with great ease climb over the said wall into his garden, and not only Robb his garden but his Mansion house, stables, and outhouses which is a very great annoyance and unsafety to him and his family.'* After this appeal the stocks were moved.

In the 18th century, Earl Camden, Chief Justice of the common pleas, when staying with an absent-minded friend, walked to an isolated common to view the stocks. Wanting to experience them, he asked his companion to fasten him in. Having done so, the man produced a book, sauntered off and forgot all about the Chief Justice. Some hours later, his lordship appealed for assistance to a farmer, who replied, *'No, old man, I guess you weren't set in 'em for nought.'*

Months afterwards, when Earl Camden was in his court, he asked a barrister who contended that the stocks were slight punishments, whether he had ever been in them. On his indignant denial, the judge replied that he had had personal experience of them and knew full well what it was like to be in such an uncomfortable and ignominious position.

The general use of the stocks died out in about the middle of the 19th century, although isolated cases of later use have been recorded.

G. C. & M. Farnell

DINTON

The stocks with, beyond the wall, Dinton Hall

TOLL-GATES AND THEIR HOUSES

TODAY WHEN most highways are free from tolls levied on those who traverse them, it is sometimes forgotten that during the last century the traveller could not go far without being barred by a turnpike gate across the road. The gate would only be opened to let him through, on payment of a toll to the gatekeeper, who emerged from his toll-house by the roadside. This was usually his place of abode. Many of these toll-houses survive along main roads. They are recognised by their proximity to the highway, and have their main doors facing on to it. In this area there are toll-houses still to be found.

Nineteenth century provincial newspapers are full of references and public notices concerning turnpike roads and their regulations and tolls chargeable. Trustees of the turnpike roads advertised for offers from those willing to take over the collection of tolls for the year, in return for a fixed annual sum. The contractor bid a sum which he reckoned would give him a fair profit after paying men to man the gates along the route.

For instance, the trustees of the Wendover to Buckingham Turnpike Trust met at the White Hart, Aylesbury, in 1834 to offer at auction for one year the tolls arising and payable at their toll-gates and side bars. The gates were put up at the following sums. Walton Gate and Side bar £700. Holman's Bridge and Weighing engine £667. Buckingham Gate and Side bar £463. These were the sums produced in the previous year over and above the expenses of collection.

An interesting court case occurred in 1868, when John Thompson was charged at Aylesbury by Mr. Tonge of the Walton Gate, with evasion of a 4½d toll for a cart laden with firewood. The defendant claimed that he was only crossing the trust road from Stoke Road into Walton Road. But he was followed and seen to go along Park Street into Bierton Road and continue round into Buckingham Road which was a further stretch of the turnpike road. Had he not gone on to the trust road again he would have been exempt from tolls. The case hinged on whether 100 yards of trust road had been covered in all. The Bench delayed judgment for a week.

Hayward Parrott

AYLESBURY
Stoke Road cottage by side bar

The Walton Gate toll-house was put up for auction in 1878 and soon afterwards demolished.

The inconvenience of the system is brought home to those who have often to drive across one or other of the dwindling number of toll-bridges which still survive.

The scale of the tolls levied can be seen by those charged at Old Stratford Bridge over the River Ouse:

For every horse or other beast drawing any coach or carriage of any kind	3d
For every horse or other beast drawing any wagon, van, cart, etc.	2d
For every horse or other beast laden or unladen and not drawing	1d
For every score of oxen, cows, or neat cattle, (calves excepted), in proportion for any less number	10d
For every score of calves, swine, sheep or lambs in proportion for less number	5d
For every carriage moved or propelled by steam or machinery or by any other power than animal power	5/-

WATERMILLS

WATERMILLS DATE back to Roman times. At the time of the Domesday Survey there were about 130 mills in Buckinghamshire, mostly on manorial estates, the tenants of which used them for grinding their grain. From early times water power was used for fulling cloth and eventually for sawing timber, paper making and so on. Many mills must have been built or enlarged during the latter part of the the 18th and early part of the 19th centuries. In 1798, the Marquis of Buckingham recorded eighty three watermills in the county.

Water power was usually more reliable than the windmill, which was subject to deadly calms or violent storms which could wreck the sails. But well-placed watermills were rarely halted for lack of a good head of water.

The Thames and its rivulets, and the Ouse in the north of the county had plenty of good sites. Many of the locks between Marlow and Oxford had mills, Hambleden being outstanding. Others, notably sawmills and paper mills, were located on the River Chess or the Misbourne, and the lower part of the Wye valley at Wycombe and Wooburn Green, or in the Colne Valley at Horton and Wraysbury.

Watermills were of three types – overshot, undershot and breast wheels, depending on situation and fall of water. Until the mid-19th century, when improvements were introduced which utilised the speed of the water flow rather than its weight, the undershot wheel was least effective.

Overshot wheels were favoured where there was a high fall of water, as they relied on the weight of water against the buckets or floats on the wheel. Breast shot wheels in time became more popular than overshot as they used the weight of water at a point about midway on the wheel, which turned in the same direction as an undershot wheel.

The teeth of the main gear wheel in watermills had to be of oak as they turned in a water filled pit. The water wheel was made of oak or cast-iron in segments and the floats were generally made in elm which survived well when

G. C. & M. Farnell

A MILL IN THE VALE

saturated with water.

Millers often met problems because other users higher upstream upset the flow of water. Boats also had to be left with sufficient depth of water to navigate. The mill was started or stopped by opening or closing a sluice, which directed the flow to the wheel or diverted it.

The Historical Monuments Commission records only three watermills built prior to 1700 which had survived in Bucks. One was at High Wycombe, possibly on the site of one of the Wycombe mills mentioned in the Domesday Survey and containing re-used timbers of early medieval date. The Town Mill at Amersham was built at the beginning of the 17th century or possibly earlier, and Lords Mill at Waterside, Chesham, was another which had survived from an early time.

Most Bucks mills employed the overshot wheel. One such was at Ellesborough mill, the rim of which was made of elm. The mill pond was supplied from a spring a quarter of a mile away. This once formed part of the Chequers Estate. The mill was burnt down about 1928.

The old *'Dunn Mill'* near Whitchurch had an iron overshot wheel 26ft. in diameter. It stood on the site of an earlier mill of wood, worked by a wooden wheel outside.

Other mid-Bucks mills were at Saunderton and Longwick near Princes Risborough. Nearby were two paper mills on the Lyde brook at Bledlow. In or round Aylesbury were Oxford Road mill, Walton mill, Broughton mill, Stoke mill, Marsh mill and Haydon mill.

North Bucks had a mill on the River Ousel near Stoke Hammond. Tingewick mill had a wooden breast wheel, the rim being of elm. This wheel, as was customary, drove two pairs of stones. Small watermills usually produced about 8 to 12 hp. Padbury claimed a 17th century mill.

The arrival of steam power heralded the end of water power except for isolated corn mills, some of which continued using the millstream to drive their wheels up to recent times. With the soaring cost of present sources of energy depending on combustion, natural power derived from wind and water may yet have a part to play.

Hayward Parrott

STOKE HAMMOND
The watermill

SOME OLD WATER PUMPS

ABOUT 1834 a Marlow resident complained that the water brought to his bedroom for daily use smelt strongly of camphor at the time of the autumn rains. He did not know if the water from his pump only had this odour or whether it was general. From the slugs and *'similar nice animals'* which he saw in it sometimes he supposed there was some connection with the river. He thought the smell arose from decaying vegetable matter in the Thames.

As water pumps were in common use in backyards of houses, and placed at convenient points on the squares or greens of towns and villages, such experiences and much graver risks to health from pollution were commonplace. A survey in 1849 reported that water drawn from a well behind an Aylesbury inn was *'at times very foul and unfit to drink, having a horrible foetid taste'*. On the other hand the pump that in 1838 had been put in the nearby open space of Kingsbury served water that was said to be very good.

Water pumps made of elm predate those constructed of iron and other metal. Elm had been used to make pumps since the idea of raising water by using a lever or a wheel had been conceived. Elm stood immersion in water for long periods. A tree might be felled on the farm to supply timber for the pump and other carpentry. Occasionally the craftsman might add slight ornamentation to the visible parts of the pump. These wooden pumps had an advantage in that they rarely froze in hard winters. Their construction is described fully in the *'Shell Book of Country Crafts'*.

In 1849 the local board of health erected six pumps in the county town. These were at Whitehall Street, Back Buckingham Street, Oxford Road (probably opposite Mount Street), Upper Hundreds, Walton Street and Castle Street. A good specimen of one of the old nineteenth-century town water pumps can be seen in Pebble Lane, Aylesbury. This pump has now a plaque explaining its origin. In 1857 it was agreed to pay £4 to keep the pumps in repair for a year.

Before World War I the old vicarage pump at Wendover survived

G. C. & M. Farnell

halfway up Back Street. Possibly one of the old houses nearby was at one time the vicarage. This pump had a little gabled roof and a stone basin to catch the surplus water. Here the local people came to fill their buckets and exchange a little idle gossip while waiting their turn.

A very old pump is found against the wall of Amersham's ancient town hall. The pump bears the date 1785, that is just over a century after the hall was built. Some pumps were upgraded by the erection of ornamental shelters enabling the drawer of water to work the pump handle under cover. Such refinements were often added later by a benefactor as a memorial to a person or national event.

Many hand-worked pumps are still used by dwellers outside the range of piped water supply. With more knowledge of the risks inherent in drinking polluted water, and closer checks on the sources of supply, these pumps raise probably a purer product. The removal of old pumps from backyards has left a legacy of old wells which have not been filled in, hence the accident that occurs from time to time when a cover placed over an old well subsides under a man's weight, precipitating him into the well beneath. If local authorities compiled registers of them some accidents might be avoided.

As one turns on the water tap, it is salutary to remember that old-time resident of Marlow who found slugs and *'similar nice animals'* in his pump water.

NORTH MARSTON
The village pump

MANY OF the 19th century workhouses, or *Union houses* as they were defined by the Poor Law Act of 1834, still stand on the outskirts of country towns. No longer needed for their original purposes, new uses have been found for their solid, and sometimes forbidding buildings which recall the sad scenes that Charles Dickens portrayed in Oliver Twist. The book was published in the late 1830's and the conditions described more likely obtained in badly adapted old buildings in the narrow streets of small towns. Cramped and overcrowded, many of these communal homes of sinister repute were pulled down when their inmates were moved into new Union houses which were erected in the mid-19th century.

Sister Sale MBE

An early Aylesbury workhouse was adjacent to the churchyard. Paupers, imbeciles, infirm, aged, wayfarers and orphans were crowded together. Male and female sleeping rooms were provided and inmates were free to wander where they pleased during daytime, but returned for meals. The original idea that they should work had almost gone. Such places were usually in charge of a caretaker and his wife who ran them on parish funds.

The number of inmates increased yearly. Parish officers often farmed out the undertaking to speculators who undertook in return for a fixed sum, to board, clothe and manage the workhouse at so much per head. In 1781, Mr. William Foreman agreed to maintain the poor of Aylesbury parish for £669 for one year. In 1825, the contract per head per week was 4/6d. £20 was later allowed the contractor for loss sustained due to an unexpected rise in food prices. In 1829 larger premises were built near Mount Street, on land given by Mr. William Rickford, the Aylesbury banker and M.P. They were superseded by the edifice which still stands in Bierton Road.

The Aylesbury Union house was erected in 1844–45, and with its entrance lodges and gables has quite a pleasing aspect. The old Board of Guardians was abolished in 1930 when responsibility was vested in the Bucks County Council. The Poor Law system was ended by the National Assistance Act, 1947. The old Aylesbury buildings are now part of Tindal General Hospital.

The former workhouse in Whielden Street, Amersham, was built in 1838 to the plans of Sir Giles Scott, in Tudor style, of flint and red brick. Today it forms part of Amersham General Hospital. In 1843, the Board of Guardians of the Amersham Union advertised for contracts in '*The Aylesbury News*'. Among the items sought were:

> *'Coffins, Shrouds, caps and pillows for all paupers dying within the Union. The coffins to be made of good sound elm board; for the persons 7 years and upwards, 1 inch thick; 1 month and under 7 years, ¾ inch thick; and under 1 month, ½ inch thick. To be well pitched inside, and to be delivered at any place within the Union where required. Prices to be stated as follows: For persons 14 years and upwards; 7 years and under 14; 1 month and under 7 years; and under 1 month.'*

Sir Giles Gilbert Scott also designed the workhouse at Winslow. This was put up in 1835. This famous architect was responsible too for the old Buckingham workhouse of the same date.

In March 1844 a group of paupers from the Aylesbury Union were shipped overseas as emigrants. In October 1844, 16 paupers were committed to gaol from Wycombe, Eton, Aylesbury and Amersham Unions, for *destroying their clothing and other offences.* Presumably this was a form of protest at conditions in the workhouses.

No doubt there were good and bad conditions, kindness and ill-treatment, in Union houses. Times were different, the public conscience was often indifferent. The guardians may have lacked understanding. The staff worked long hours carrying out tasks which were often unpleasant and squalid. Perhaps it is as well that these buildings have served their purpose. Many of them foster new projects of learning and administer to human welfare in wider fields.

IN CONCLUSION I think that the publishers, Kylin Press, in the person of Gerry Tomlinson, Geoff Apps, the designer and Hazell, Watson & Viney Limited, the printers, have between them produced rather a nice book to have on one's bookshelves. The tireless efforts of Gerry in locating sources of illustration, some of it hitherto unpublished, and the willing co-operation of so many in making the material in their charge available, has been invaluable.

I greatly hope that those who have read this book from cover to cover will feel that it has been worthwhile and will treasure it over the years, so that those of younger generations may also enjoy 'Aylesbury Vale Yesterdays'.

H.P.

Back endpaper:
THE VALE OF AYLESBURY
from Barrack Hill, above Lower Winchendon
G. C. & M Farnell
1965